Praying for Your Job

Books by Elmer L. Towns and Dave Earley

Praying for Your Children

Available from Destiny Image Publishers

Praying for Your Job

Prosperity, Fulfillment, Happiness

Elmer L. Towns and Dave Earley

DESTINY IMAGE® PUBLISHERS, INC.

P.O. Box 310, Shippensburg, PA 17257-0310

"Speaking to the Purposes of God for This Generation and for the Generations to Come."

This book and all other Destiny Image, Revival Press, MercyPlace, Fresh Bread, Destiny Image Fiction, and Treasure House books are available at Christian bookstores and distributors worldwide.

For a U.S. bookstore nearest you, call **1-800-722-6774.**

For more information on foreign distributors, call **717-532-3040.**

Reach us on the Internet: **www.destinyimage.com.**

ISBN Trade Paper: 978-0-7684-3674-7

ISBN Ebook: 978-0-7684-9029-9

For Worldwide Distribution, Printed in the U.S.A.

2 3 4 5 6 7 8 / 15 14 13 12 11

Contents

Introduction

WORK; some people love it, others hate it, but most people need work to pay the bills and keep life going.

Work; some are good at it, others are sloppy, while others are just terrible workers; but most people still go to work on a regular basis because they need the paycheck.

Work; some feel trapped in a low-paying job or a job in miserable conditions, while others feel they are making a significant contribution, or they rapidly move up the economic ladder.

Work; some can't wait for the closing whistle to go home, or they live for retirement, while others joyfully put in extra hours without extra pay to get a job done, and they don't plan to retire because they love what they do.

Work; some are known by their job, such as a salesperson, contractor, or bus driver; while others are embarrassed by their job and never get around to telling people where they work.

If you hate your work or think it's below your dignity, remember the first picture we see in the Bible is God working, *"In the beginning God created the heavens and the earth"* (Gen. 1:1). Then, *"God ended His work which He had done"* (Gen. 2:2).

Because we are made in the image and likeness of God, why shouldn't we work just as God worked? Of course we do different kinds of work and on a much lower level, but the point is—we should work because God worked.

Your Acquired Task

Therefore, look at your job—or work—as an acquired duty that you must do because you are made in God's image. Just as all students are given homework, and all employees are given tasks, because you were made in the image of God, you have been assigned the task of working (verb) or a job (noun).

Lord, I will work at my job with new zeal because I realize You worked, and You have given me the privilege of working. I repent of the sour attitude I have toward my work; give me an overriding new attitude toward my work. Amen.

God's Plan for You

God wants us to live healthy, productive lives that glorify Him. Therefore, God allowed you to be born into a family that will have great influence over where you live, what you eat, how you live, and where you work.

Have you ever realized God has a plan for *where* you work, *how* you work, and what your job will accomplish in your life, as well as the lives of others? God influenced your workplace by giving you to your parents. Therefore, through your parents God prepared you for life and by placing you in a specific culture, influenced your attitudes toward work.

You had no control over the choice of your parents or your culture. But you do have a choice over the quality of your work, the faithfulness of your work, and the productivity of your work. In this sense: *"We are God's fellow workers"* (1 Cor. 3:9).

Lord, thank You for what I've learned from my parents and home; and thank You for the positive influence of my culture. I will work hard and faithfully at my job to glorify You. Give me strength and wisdom to do better than I've ever done before. Amen.

Your Work Is Your Craftsmanship

Your work expresses who you are, and the quality of your work reflects your character. In one sense, you are only as good as the effort you put into your work. Your workmanship reflects who you are in life. So pray that God will lead you to a job where your talents can be used. Find a job where your greatest contribution to life can be made. If you're not in that job now, begin praying to find that job, and ask God to help you "land" that job.

Lord, I want fulfillment in the work I do, and I want to fulfill all my boss wants of me. I will do my best at all times in all ways. I will learn and grow to the utmost of my abilities. I want the "things" I do at work to reflect the quality of character I feel in my heart. Amen.

Your Work Sculptures Your Character

God gives us work for several reasons. First, God gives us work so we can make a contribution to society in general and to our family specifically. But God probably has a second greater reason for work. Work provides challenges, discipline, and growth. Work molds us into better citizens in our society, better members of our family, and better servants of God.

Because you're a Christian, you ought to work harder and better than you would have without Christ. But also, God gives you a job to mold you into His image—into well-rounded perfection. The old King James version of the Bible used the word *perfection* for the newer word *maturity* (see Matt. 5:48; Eph. 4:12-13).

We are like blocks of marble from which God, the Sculptor, wants to carve us into a beautiful sculpture (God is the Master who shapes us into the masterpiece). So God uses work to make us do the things we don't want to do, or we think we can't. But we usually get the job done, and we grow in maturity in the process. Our work shapes us into the finished sculpture that God wants us to become.

Lord, forgive me when I complain about my work, and don't punish me for backing away from hard jobs. Give me courage to face impossible jobs. Give me wisdom to solve problems that seem insolvable. Give me strength to do tasks that are too hard. Give me patience to keep working when it looks like I can't get it done. And as I strive, grow my character to be more like Christ. Amen.

Your Work Opens Doors

Think of all the people you encounter in the workplace. There are many people you wouldn't have met if it wasn't for your job. Charles "Tremendous" Jones said, "All you will be five years from now is a result of the people you meet and the books you read."[1] Therefore, meeting people at work will grow your character.

You will meet many non-Christians on the job. Because you're a Christian, you can help them through their problems of life and perhaps even lead them to Christ.

Only in Heaven will you realize how much you've grown because of your job, and only in Heaven will you realize how much God was leading you to a job, and how God was using you on your job. And when in Heaven, you will realize all the lives you've touched at your place of work; and you'll realize how much others have caused you to grow in Christ.

Lord, thank You for all the jobs I've had in the past, and thank You for my present job. Teach me through my job. Let me help others I meet through my work and let them help me. Use my work experience to make me more like You. Amen.

Work is one of the greatest contributions to your life. Think about it! It's better for God to give you work than to give you money that you don't work for. You will enjoy your possessions much more when you work for them than if they were given to you without your effort. Work is a gift from God. Accept your job gratefully. Thank God for your employment. Pray for your spiritual growth through work, and use your employment to glorify God.

Written from our homes at the foot of the Blue Ridge Mountains,

Elmer L. Towns, Cofounder
Liberty University

David Earley
Chairman of Pastoral Leadership
Liberty Baptist Theological Seminary

Endnote

1. See Charles "Tremendous" Jones Motivational Quotes, available at http://www.inspirational-motivational-speakers.com/CharlesTremendousJonesQuotes.html (accessed November 2, 2009).

Section I

Your First Reaction

Chapter 1

How to Pray to Find a Job

Elmer Towns

Find something you love to do and you'll never have to work a day in your life. —Harvey MacKay

You have not because you ask not (James 4:2).

BECAUSE you're a Christian, you begin looking for a job at a different place from where the world looks. You begin with God, whereas the world begins someplace else.

A young kid who just graduated from high school might begin looking in the employment section of the newspaper, or he asks his friends, or he keeps his eyes open for a "help wanted" sign in any of the stores he visits.

A good way to find a job is to ask around among your friends, maybe they know someplace that is hiring, or they have a relative who can help; don't forget contacts.

Then think about open positions that are never advertised or maybe you'll never see a "help wanted" sign advertising it. Why? Because there are employers who don't want to be bothered with a lot of interviews, nor do they want to bother themselves with sifting through a lot of chaff just to find one needle in a haystack. There are employers who don't fill an empty spot—they get along with the employees they have—they are waiting for the right person to come along. These employers tell their contacts, and in turn these people tell their contacts. Pretty soon, the right person searching for a job meets a "contact" who talks to the employer about you.

Then there are other ways that people find jobs. Sometimes jobs are posted at the unemployment office, or in the personnel and/or human relations office of large companies. Sometimes opportunities are posted on the Internet or in magazines. As an illustration, a college may post its need for a professor in a professional journal.

A Christian can and should pray about all these possibilities, but a Christian has other assets the world doesn't have. Christians have God on their side. But the Christian must begin by getting on God's side. It all begins when you realize, "God has a plan for my life."

Lord, when I forget about You, remind me that You care about me. Remind me to pray and seek Your will for my life. Lord, remind me that You are more concerned about my next job than I am. Lord, I come to You. Amen.

Start Your Job Search With God

Before reading the help wanted ads, looking around town for a job, or doing anything, Christians must understand that they belong to God and that the Lord has a plan for their lives.

After my freshman year at Columbia Bible College, I took a job at Ben Lippen Camp near Asheville, North Carolina. I arrived a week early to clean the facilities that had been closed all winter. I was one of three boys who were cleaning the camp. After the evening meal, my two partners went to bed because they were tired. We were supposed to hose down and mop the dining hall that day, and it had not been done. So around nine o'clock at night I found myself without any help, with my jeans rolled up to my knees, splashing a hose of water and mopping up the large dining hall. It had open screens on three sides. I tell you that to let you know that it was really dirty with the wind blowing in dirt all winter.

I was complaining about the two boys who didn't feel an obligation to finish their task that day. I pushed my mop up to the middle of the floor where a blue sign read, "GOD HAS A PLAN FOR YOUR LIFE."

I rested my chin on the end of the mop, looked at the sign and laughed to myself, *Is it God's plan for me to work while my buddies sleep?*

Then it dawned on me that I had something better than my two friends, I had character and commitment. I was going to finish the job that was given to me that day. They were non-finishers. Some might call them quitters.

Then a second thought hit me, *Lord, is Your plan for me to mop floors all my life?*

I had great plans I wanted to do for God, but it dawned on me that night that, *If I do everything today to the best of my ability, God will take care of my tomorrows....*

I meditated on that sign a long while before going back to work; as a matter of fact, it was like having my devotions before I got back to my cabin.

GOD—The Lord of Heaven, was ruling my life.

HAS—My life's plan was not for some future event, but for that place and that time. God had a plan for me that day and it was to do the best job I could with mopping the floor.

A PLAN—That didn't mean God controlled every small detail of my life, but He had an overall plan, and I had the responsibility to fulfill my task in that plan. I determined to do the best job possible mopping the floor.

FOR—God's plan was not for the universe, or for everyone else, but God's plan was for ME.

YOUR LIFE—God was not concerned with just my thinking, or my feeling, God was concerned with my total life. That night I yielded to God to find His plan and do it as best I could.

So as you look for a job, you should take the same attitude that I took. You should pray this prayer:

Lord, You have a plan for my life, and I yield myself to find it and do it. I will seek Your plan for my life and give all my energy to find Your plan. Then I will do Your plan for my life. Amen.

Pray for God to Guide You Into His Will

And what is prayer? It is simply a relationship with God whereby you talk with God and listen to Him as He speaks to you. Prayer is the greatest asset that a Christian has; because by prayer, a Christian gets God on his side.

Therefore, before you begin looking for a job, ask God to help you find that job. Notice, I say "help" you find that job. Don't treat prayer as a crutch, whereby you wait for God to find and deliver a job to you. No! You must actively seek a job using all of your intellect, energy, and instinct.

Let's come back to prayer. Jesus said, *"And whatever you ask in My name, that I will do…"* (John 14:13). In another place He said, *"Ask and it will be given to you; seek, and you will find; knock, and it will be opened to you"* (Matt. 7:7). So, asking is the rule around God's house, therefore ask Him to help you find a job.

So when you begin praying, follow these three steps. First of all, ask God to make you keenly aware as you search for a job, to understand what you see and to not miss any important item in a job posting.

Lord, give me eyes to see potential jobs where I could work. Amen.

Second, pray for God to give you wisdom to match up your abilities with the job's demand. It's useless to apply for a job that is beyond your capacities. Also, would you want a job that is far below your ability?

Third, ask God to lead you in the application process. You will need divine guidance in filling out the application, presenting the application, and the interview process.

Lord, help me make a good impression when I apply for a job. Amen.

If God helps you in all of these, it is more than likely that you will get the job rather than being turned down.

Lord, lead me to talk to the right people about work opportunities. When I fill out an application, help me say the right thing in the right way. Help me understand the one(s) who will interview me, then help me wear the appropriate clothing, and say the correct thing to get the job. Lord, work through the little things to help me get the job You want me to have. Then after I've done the little things correctly, do a big thing for me: give me a job. Amen.

Eight Keys to Finding a Job

1. Get the word out. The more people who know you're looking, the more likely you'll find a job.

2. Find out where people with your background are working. Find companies that employ people like you by doing an advanced search for people in your area who have your skills.

3. Find out where people at a company came from.

4. Find out where people from a company go next.

5. Get to the hiring manager.

6. Get to the right HR person.

7. Find out the secret job requirements. Find a connection at the company who can get the inside scoop on what really matters for the job.

8. Build your network before you need it.[1]

Pray About God's Will as You Study His Word

As a believer, you are seeking the will of God for your life. Remember, the will of God can be a "verb" or a "noun." When we say God's will is a "verb," it means this is God's choice, or what God has decided for you. So pray that you will be within God's decision.

Next, the will of God is a "noun" meaning it is a plan or blueprint for your life. At this place, the will of God is like a daily schedule of work, one schedule for each day for the rest of your life.

Remember, the will of God and the Word of God are consistent. Therefore, look at all jobs through the Scriptures. That means some jobs you cannot take because it might compromise your Christian life and witness. The Ten Commandments tell you to not lie, nor steal, nor commit adultery, nor to covet (be greedy) anything that belongs to your neighbor. Because God's will is found in God's Word, that means you turn down jobs that require you to exaggerate the truth (lie) or actually take money illegally; this also rules out gambling, or anything associated with gambling, or any job where you are required to misrepresent the truth.

Because God prohibits a believer from giving strong drink to another (see Prov. 20:1 and Hab. 2:15), you cannot take a job as a bartender or sell alcohol. A Christian cannot have anything to do with illicit sex, pornography, or any industry that leads to adultery.

There's another thing about prayer. When you're praying for outward things about your job, don't forget to pray about your inner conformity to the will of God. If you were to pray the Lord's Prayer daily, you would ask, "Thy will be done." That means each day you ask for God's will to be done in your life.

But more than asking for a job, you must ask to be conformed to the image of Jesus Christ (see Rom. 8:28-29). That means, you pray to become more like Jesus every day of your life, so you ask God to give you a job that will help you reach that goal.

Lord, I will study Your Word to know Your will for my life. I want to be in the very center of Your will and fulfill Your plan for my life. Amen.

YIELD YOURSELF TO GOD IN PRAYER

Sometimes we begin a job search with one task in mind, and we miss other good jobs because we are not open to opportunities that are different from the task we seek. Maybe God wants you to do something other than your passion. Maybe God wants you to yield to Him first; and once you surrender to His will, God can lead you to the job He wants you to have.

When I was in Bible college, a missionary speaker once said from the platform, "*The thing you don't want to do is God's will for your life.*" That sounded like good advice to me, and I began to think of the things I didn't want to do. While thinking about it, I looked down the row and saw a girl I just didn't like. Then the thought hit me, "You don't want to marry her, so that must be God's will for your life!"

No...no...no...I completely rejected any thoughts of marrying that girl. I sat through chapel in panic, thinking God wants me to marry that girl. I kept thinking to myself, *The thing you don't want to do is God's will for your life.*

"*Therefore yield…*" The chapel speaker kept driving home the fact I had to yield to God and do the things I didn't want to do. I was yielded to God, yet I struggled with my "rejection of that girl," and couldn't get peace for approximately a week.

About a week later a young missionary lady from South America said, "If you are yielded to God, then what you want to do may be God's will for you."

These words were like soothing ointment on a raw sore. I felt I was yielded to God, but still didn't want to marry that particular girl. Suddenly the whole issue of "yieldedness" unfolded in my mind. From then on I had peace about the issue.

So put these two things together. If you are unyielded to God, what you don't want to do may be God's will. On the other hand, if you are yielded to God, what you want to do may be God's will for your life.

Therefore, as you pray for a job, ask yourself the question, "Am I yielded to God?" And follow up with the second question, "Am I willing to take whatever job God gives me?" When you get the right answer to both of these questions, you are ready to search for the job God has for you.

Lord, I yield myself to You, and with that I yield my desires and preferences for a job. I yield my lifelong dreams for employment. Help me see Your will for my life, and then guide me through my search, my contacts, my applications, and through circumstances to find the job You have for me. If I'm looking for the wrong type of job, redirect my efforts. If I'm looking in the wrong place, refocus my search. If I have the wrong attitude to get a job, transform my attitude. Amen.

Pray for God to Help You Find Your Spiritual Gifts

The Bible teaches, *"Each one has his proper gift of God"* (1 Cor. 7:7 ELT). Your "proper gift" is your spiritual ability to serve God. We are told in Scripture, *"Each one should use their gift as they have received it, serving one another as good stewards of the grace of God"* (1 Pet. 4:10 ELT). Our serving gifts, or spiritual gifts, that are mentioned in the Bible are really our talents or abilities. God has gifted to each of us with different talents or abilities to serve in this life, and by using our abilities properly, we are serving the Lord.

Some people are good with their hands, and so they should seek a job where they have to use their physical abilities. Some people are good figuring out answers to difficult problems, and they should find a job where their creativity can be used. What about those who are good at human relations? They should find a job where they deal with people and the success of their job depends on good relations with people.

Therefore, before you begin to file job applications at every opening in your town, you ought to fill out a spiritual gift inventory. Visit www.elmertowns.com, find the "Spiritual Gift Test," and take the spiritual gift test (it will take about 15 minutes). Find your strengths, and then ask God to lead you to a position where you can use your strengths to His glory.

Many think that only preachers or missionaries should pray about a job, or these are the people who should be concerned about spiritual gifts. That is not true. Every Christian should be led of the Lord to find work opportunities. So every Christian should try to use their spiritual gifts to fulfill their work opportunities. You don't have God's second best if you don't go into full-time Christian service.

Lord, help me to properly understand myself and my gifts and talents. May I see my strengths and weaknesses more clearly than I've ever seen them before. Then, Lord, help me "match" my abilities to the job market and available positions. Lead me to apply for the right openings, and help me honestly and accurately present my abilities to a prospective employer. Lord, give me a job that best uses the abilities You've given me. Amen.

Pray for God to Guide You as You Counsel With Spiritually Mature Friends

The Bible teaches, *"Many counsels bring success"* (Prov. 15:22 TLB). Again it says, *"With many counselors, there is safety"* (Prov. 11:14 TLB).

Sometimes a friend may say to you, "Why don't you try this line of work?" Maybe that friend sees something in you that you can't see in yourself. Sometimes your ego is so wrapped up with your desires that you can't see your abilities. But when a friend gives you good counsel, you may find God's plan and a job for your life.

I felt God calling me to serve Him full-time immediately after my conversion. I felt God wanted me in full-time Christian service, but I didn't know where. While in my senior year in college, Dr. Ed Simpson, my Bible teacher, was used of God to focus my direction in life. I was giving a report on an exegetical passage in First Peter when Dr. Simpson said, "Elmer, you do an excellent job handling the Word, you ought to be a teacher in a Bible college after you finish seminary...."

I knew I liked to teach the Word, and what he said reconfirmed that plan for my life. Here is what you should pray:

Lord, lead me to a friend or person who can best help me get a job. If this is a person I've never met, lead me to this person and help me see how this person can help me. Lord, help me be a friend to all. Help me look at life through the eyes of my friends, and help them look at my life through my eyes. Lord, give me someone to help me. Amen.

Pray for God to Guide Your Job Search as You Apply Common Sense

Technically, God holds us responsible for the decisions we make, and the way we direct our lives. Solomon tells us, *"We make our plans, but the Lord determines our steps"* (Prov. 16:9 ELT). That means we think through all the options as we make plans for the future, but the Lord is behind the scenes guiding the steps we take.

Very seldom does God lead a person contrary to common sense. And what is common sense? It has been called many things in life.

The old farmer calls it "horse sense," the wife calls it, "mother's wit;" it is also known as "practical knowledge," "shrewdness," or "gumption." However, when you follow your common sense, you are looking at all your options, using all the wisdom and lessons you've learned in life.

However, there is a downside to common sense. We can be deceived by our inner nature because that is where lust is located. Jesus said, *"From the heart comes evil thoughts, murders, adulteries, all other sexual immoralities, theft, lying, and slander"* (Matt. 15:19 NLT). These terrible evils *can* come from within, if we don't guard our thoughts. But a disciplined Christian heart will overcome these evil thoughts. Therefore, anytime you apply common sense to a job search, make sure to check your decisions with the Word of God. If anytime your common sense contradicts the Bible, your common sense is not God's way of looking at the decision.

Lord, I will use my plain, everyday common sense when seeking a job. I know myself better than anyone else, and I know what I can do. So Lord, speak to me through my common sense. But sometimes I have been wrong in the past, so I realize I can be wrong in the future. Open my spiritual eyes to see myself more clearly than ever before. Keep me from following my common sense when it comes from the lust of my heart and will lead me away from Your will. Amen.

Common Sense

1. Common sense is the application of all the knowledge you've learned to all the problems that face you in life.

2. Common sense is seeing things as they are, and doing things as they should be done.[2]

3. Common sense is the master of human life.[3]

4. Common sense is being sensible about common things.[4]

5. Common sense is not so common.[5]

PRAY FOR GOD TO GUIDE YOU THROUGH CIRCUMSTANCES

There are many circumstances that will prepare you for a job. Like it or not, your parents will open certain doors for you simply because you are their children. The same with your family name and at other times your geographic location qualifying you for a job, and still at other times, your ethnic background will open opportunities for you.

Opportunities are called open doors. But the existence of open doors also means there will be closed doors in your life. Sometimes the job you want may be more suitable for a woman, and not you; or vice versa if you're a woman. Therefore, certain doors may be closed to you because of gender, and other doors may be closed to you because of age, or some physical limitation. For example, people in wheelchairs cannot work on an assembly line where they need to crawl in and out of cars being assembled. But the wheelchair may be an open door to others, because they have an active mind and can sit at a desk taking care of business.

I became Dean of Liberty Baptist Theological Seminary in 1979. The previous dean had not allowed any divorced person into the seminary because of his religious views. I respected his views, but changed the rule to allow divorced people into the seminary. I announced to all seminarians that certain churches would not ordain people who are divorced; neither would they call them as a pastor or leader of their church. But at the same time, I announced that there are churches that will take a divorced person.

Then I said the most important thing, "If you are divorced, don't go through life knocking on closed doors. You will be bound to a life of frustration. Forget about the closed doors and churches that won't employ a divorced person. Go through life looking for open doors where you are welcomed and you can be effective in ministry."

The same can be said about your job. Some jobs are closed to you because of lack of education, skill, physical limitations, gender, or other limitations. Don't spend your life in frustration knocking on closed doors. Find open doors, walk through them, and serve God as best you can.

Let's talk about wrong self-perceptions. Maybe you think that a certain job is beneath you, but when you get hungry, you might love a job that is beneath you simply because it will put food on the table. If a job is available, and you can't find anything else, maybe it's God's will for you to take that job.

If you've been a manager of a large factory, you may think it's beneath your dignity to be a crossing guard for children on their way to school. But if your retirement plan doesn't provide enough income and times are hard and a depression threatens, maybe a crossing guard position will keep bill collectors from the door.

Paul understood opportunities and circumstances. He wrote to the Christians at Corinth, *"For there is a wide open door for a great work here, and many people are responding"* (1 Cor. 16:9 ELT). Paul understood that when the fire is hot, you have to strike. And in the same way, when a job opening comes, you have to move quickly to get it. So learn to pray:

> *Lord, give me eyes to see opportunities and open doors. Give me a wise mind to understand the nature of open doors, and give me an inquiring curiosity to ask the right questions about open doors. Lord, help me read properly the circumstances of life, and respond properly so that I may find a job where I can serve You. Amen.*

God's Will Is Shown to Those Who Are Actively Serving Him

It's amazing how spiritual some people get when they get laid off, or when they are seeking another job. They haven't been going to church, nor have they served God; and in addition, they have not paid their tithes to God. As soon as they get laid off, they begin to pray and beg God to give them a job. Obviously, they can repent and God will hear their prayer and forgive their sins. *"If we confess our sins He is faithful and just to forgive us our sins and cleanse us from all unrighteousness"* (1 John 1:9).

But what about you? If you stay in good relationship with God all the time, you don't have to repent. You don't have to worry whether your previous complacency is being punished or not. God shows Himself to His children who are actively searching for Him.

David knew how to pray aggressively for God's will, he said, "*My heart has heard You say, 'Come and talk with me.' My heart responds, 'Lord, I am coming. Do not hide Yourself from me. Do not reject Your servant in anger. You have always been my helper. Don't leave me; don't abandon me, O God of my salvation!*'" (Ps. 27:8-9 NLT). When we seek God in prayer, He shows Himself to us first, then He shows us His will.

If you are looking for a job, this is how you should pray:

Lord, I will aggressively seek Your will first in my life. Then I will aggressively seek any job opportunities that I find. Lord, open up doors and show me opportunities that are available. Give me wisdom to see what I can do and what I can't do. Lord, show me how to apply for a job; and God, go before me to prepare the hearts of those who will interview me. God, I need employment; help me in my time of need. Amen.

QUESTIONS FOR THOUGHT

1. What's the most important thing a person must know about herself or himself when seeking a new job?

2. Where does a person begin when looking for a new job?

3. Should people take a new job just because there is a paycheck, even if it's a job they know they can't fill, or it's a job beneath them, or one that can't pay their present bills?

4. How important is it for a people to know their spiritual gifts when looking for a job?

5. How important is "common sense" when looking for a job?

6. How important is "prayer" in finding a job? How can God help you find a job that you can't find yourself?

ENDNOTES

1. "How to Change the World," February 2, 2009, http://blog.guykawasaki.com/2009/02/10-ways-to-use.html (accessed March 26, 2009).

2. Unknown source, http://en.proverbia.net/citastema.asp?tematica=207 (accessed March 26, 2009).

3. Unknown source, http://en.proverbia.net/citastema.asp?tematica=207 (accessed March 26, 2009).

4. Unknown source, http://en.proverbia.net/citastema.asp?tematica=207 (accessed March 26, 2009).

5. Voltaire (1694–1778) French writer and historian, see http://en.proverbia.net/citastema.asp?tematica=207 (accessed March 26, 2009).

Chapter 2

How to Pray When You Think You May Lose Your Job

Elmer Towns

The best way to appreciate your job is to imagine yourself without one. —Oscar Wilde

Fear not, for I am with you (Isaiah 41:10).

SOME people go to work every day thinking that they'll get the "pink slip" and Friday will be their last day. Perhaps they're neurotic, pessimistic, or they're the kind of person with little confidence. Is that you?

Other people are blindsided. They walk in thinking they have a job for life, and they've never once thought they'd be laid off. Then they're called in to the supervisor's office and told that "today is your last day."

What should be the attitude of a Christian toward being laid off? Perhaps it is somewhere between being neurotic and being so confident that one day you're blindsided. No matter your attitude toward your work, you must have a completely different attitude when it comes to God.

The following steps are suggested, although they are not in the perfect sequence for every person who is facing job termination. Perhaps you've never worried about being laid off; but even for you, some of these steps should be followed.

Be Confident in Your Job for Today

You may be injured and can't work, or there may be financial reversals for your company, or a number of other situations that would cause you to be terminated. You can't live in a world of "what ifs." You live today in the world of "now."

If you go to work confident, and you work with great assurance, you will do more for your job than you ever dreamed. If you're a salesperson, your confidence might help you make the "sale" of the century. If you are a manager, your assurance may help you solve one of the biggest crises in your company. No matter what your position, when you work with confidence perhaps your boss may see it on the day when he's making his final decision, and your confidence wins the day. He keeps you, and lays off someone else.

When the Bible says, *"Being confident of this very thing…"* (Phil. 1:6), it's regarding our salvation. But then again, doesn't the way we live for Christ daily affect our productivity at work?

Today, Do Right

If you have doubts about being terminated, this is not the time to retaliate, get angry, or spread rumors about the management. And obviously for the Christian, this is not the time to commit "white collar crime" to take home what you think belongs to you.

If today is the last day of your job, you ought to turn in the best productivity on your last day. Why? Because you don't primarily work for your boss, nor do you work primarily to please yourself—you work for Jesus Christ. *"And whatever you do or say, let it be as a representative of the Lord Jesus..."* (Col. 3:17 TLB).

As much as you work for your company, you have a greater boss—Jesus Christ. If you are a child of God, you should realize that the Lord gave you this job and He will get you the next job. Even beyond your job, the Lord can take care of you. So, when you do *right*, you have the blessing of God shining on you.

At this place, the word *repentance* should be discussed. If you've been doing something wrong, you should repent and do right. Perhaps you have a nagging doubt about some of the things you do. Now is the time to face it honestly, and make sure you do right. The person who does right, *"even makes his enemies to be at peace with him"* (Prov. 16:7).

TAKE AN INVENTORY

There is some reason why you think you're going to be terminated. You need to ask yourself the following questions and honestly face the answers.

Is the problem the economy?

Is the problem instability at work?

Is the problem financial instability of the company?

Is your job no longer necessary in a changing culture and advancement of modern times (those who made buggy whips and manual typewriters should have seen termination coming)?

Has technology passed you by?

Are you equipped or trained to do your job?

Do you have an attitude problem, i.e., are you constantly angry at your boss or other employees?

Are you slacking off on the job and not giving it your best?

Have you been there so long that you are taking advantage of company policies and priorities?

The answer to any of the above questions may help you understand why you have doubts about your employment. When you have a good idea what the problem might be, you may be able to fix it. You may be able to work harder, take a class, or do other things to make you more productive to your company.

There are some things that can't be fixed. If progress has passed your company by, you may have to find a company that has a new and better "mouse trap."

There are some other questions you might ask, such as when will an electric car make the gasoline car obsolete? Sometimes it is not just about praying about your job, the issue is being smart enough to see the facts and analyze what you have to do.

Even then, pray that God would give you wisdom to understand and courage to act on what you *know*.

Deal With Your Fears

In one sense, many people have fears about their job. Perhaps they know their company is struggling financially, so they wonder how long their job is going to last. You have to deal with your fears.

First, it's wrong to trust in money, and that includes your retirement fund, life insurance, or unemployment benefits. Jesus told us, *"Do not lay up for yourselves treasures on earth"* (Matt. 6:19). Then He went on to say that we should *"lay up for yourselves treasures in heaven"* (Matt. 6:20). That means we should not worry about money, but look beyond the money God gives to us to our relationship with Him.

Quickly let us say it's not wrong to have a retirement fund, life insurance, or social security. There were people in the Bible who had money to take care of themselves as Abraham and his sons and David and his sons. It's not wrong to have money, it's wrong to let money own you.

Jesus said, *"For where your treasure is, there your heart will be also"* (Matt. 6:21). What does He mean by this? If our basic commitment in life is money, then that's what our lives are wrapped up in. And if your life is wrapped up in money, it is kind of hard to pray to God to take care of you. Why should He take care of you when you use your money to take care of yourself?

It's Always Right to be Concerned About Your Job

You have someone depending on you, and perhaps your children need their necessities met by your job. And what about your mate? Is there someone who depends upon your paycheck? So you have a right to pray and ask God to take care of you and them.

It's Right to Want to Work

If you are in good health, then you should have a desire to work that extends your creativity and contribution to life.

Please God in All You Do

Make it your desire to serve God in your work and please Him in all you do. That means down to the smallest details, you want to please God.

Pray for Your Company's Profitability and Growth in Every Area

This is more than praying for your contribution to the company, it's more than just praying for your job. Get the larger picture—pray for the president of the company, vice presidents, and all the managers. Get used to calling them by name before God. And if you pray for them:

+ Pray for their wisdom and decision-making.

+ Pray for their understanding and interpretation of the times.

+ Pray for their ability to lead.

+ Pray for their faith personally, and that they would come to know Jesus Christ as Savior.

Do more than just say, "God bless my company." You'll want to tell God in what areas to bless and how to bless. Pray explicitly about the problems facing your company. The more knowing you pray, the better understanding you'll have for your company and what its needs are. As a result, you'll be a better employee.

YIELD TO GOD

Yielding may be something you're fighting, or it's something you thought about but actually have never done. Every Christian should give his life to God, and he must please God first and foremost—before he pleases his employer or anyone else. For when you please God, that means to please Him you will work harder, so you ultimately will please your boss. Make sure your priority is right: God first; employer second.

> No one can serve two masters. For you will hate one and love the other; you will be devoted to one and despise the other. You cannot serve both God and money (Matthew 6:24 NLT).

When you have your allegiances in order, then you will not be a double-minded person; you will be single-purposed in life. Hence, you will be more valuable to your company.

LOOK BEYOND ECONOMIC CONDITIONS

Remember the New York Stock Exchange didn't exist a couple of hundred years ago, but many people had good jobs and took care of their family. In the same way, the Internet didn't exist 20 years ago. Then, probably, the product that your company turns out didn't exist a hundred years ago. What does that mean?

Many people had good jobs before all these things came about, and they lived a good life. That means that "things come and go," but God continues forever. So when we ask you to "trust God," we're asking you to look beyond the parameters of this life, look to God, and look to your calling in life.

REST IN GOD

In one sense, we should not rest in our own effort, but rest in God. Jesus said: *"So don't worry about these things, saying, 'What will we eat? What will we drink? What will we wear?'"* (Matt. 6:31 NLT).

The most important thing is to rest in God and let Him take care of these things. Did you see the next verse? *"...Your heavenly Father already knows all your needs"* (Matt. 6:32 NLT).

Since God knows about these things, when you pray to remind Him, you are asking God to open the door to supply your needs. God can take care of you when you are "in prosperity" or when you're in "a recession." God is in the business of taking care of people, we have to make it our business to trust Him.

LOOK TO YOUR SUPPORT GROUP

Your group may or may not be people with whom you pray. Your support group are those who love and care for you. Let them know what's happening to you.

So first of all, look to your friends at work. Get their reading of your situation, and listen to their comments. Sometimes when it appears you are losing your job, friends will tell you things that they wouldn't have told you before. In an emergency, people step forward with information that you will need.

Next, look to your support group at home; this involves your spouse, your children, and relatives. Don't forget your own father and mother, if they are still living. These people can help, and you need to look at life through their lives.

Don't forget your friends; these are those you fellowship with, attend sporting events with, or just others or those at your church, bowling league, or any other place they gather. These people can help you look at life through their lives. And what you see may be encouraging and give you an idea what's coming next.

Pray for Your Next Place of Work and Your Next Paycheck

Even when you have a job, there may come a time when you will be moving on. That may be next month, next year, or ten years from now. Ask God to prepare you for the next place where you will serve; ask God to prepare the place, and then at the right time put you and the place together.

Remember, God is standing at the location where you will work ten years from now. God *"calls those things which do not exist as though they did"* (Rom. 4:17). He knows your future problems and work-mates, as well as your productivity and goals. God knows everything, so trust in Him.

Pray for Spiritual Victory

The very fact that you have anxiety shows that you're not completely at rest. So pray for God to give you victory over your anxiety, or at least victory over your pessimism.

When looking to victory, thank God before you get it. Paul told us: *"But thank God! He has made us His captives and continues to lead us along in Christ's triumphal procession"* (2 Cor. 2:14 NLT).

And what is our victory? *"This is the victory that has overcome the world—our faith"* (1 John 5:4). This means that the very nature of our victory comes from our faith. We must have faith in God to lead us, provide for us, and look after our needs.

Recommit Yourself to Spiritual Discipline

No matter who we are in life or what situation we are in life, we should always come back to our spiritual discipline. Jesus told us: *"But seek first the kingdom of God and His righteousness, and all these things shall be added to you"* (Matt. 6:33).

The word *first* means God is your priority. It means put God's plan for your life first.

So come back to the place of seeking God in the Scriptures. You must commit yourself to say, "I will read the Scriptures…."

Then you must commit yourself to a daily relationship to God through prayer. You come to the place where you will say, "I will seek God in prayer daily…."

And then you have to make sure that your church has the right place in your life. You come to the place where you say, "I will serve Jesus Christ through the local church...."

So what are you doing? You are strengthening your relationship with God, and from that place of power you are able to cope with whatever comes. Whether you are terminated or promoted, God will help you through the ordeal.

Lord, give me confidence about my job. I will work hard to fulfill expectations by my superiors, help them see my dedication and accomplishments. Give me a good evaluation in the eyes of my superior. If I've done something wrong to get a "bad" evaluation or to get in my boss' "dog house," help me realize what I've done. Show me how to correct my faults, failures, and my wrong attitude. Lord, protect me and my job. I will work to please You. Amen.

Questions for Thought

1. In what ways can people know they are in danger of losing their job?

2. When people think they are going to lose their job, what can they do to turn around a "deteriorating" situation?

3. How can a person lay out a plan to make himself more valuable to his boss or to the company?

4. How can a person with a "bad attitude" at work, turn her attitude around so that she develops a "good attitude" about work?

5. How can a person prepare himself for the "meeting," when he is informed that he is being released?

6. What are some of the things a person should do in relationship to her previous "company" when she is released?

7. What are the things a person should do after the loss of his or her job?

Chapter 3

How to Pray When You Lose Your Job

Elmer Towns

*Never continue in a job you don't enjoy. If you're happy
in what you're doing, you'll like yourself, you'll have inner
peace. And if you have that, along with physical health,
you will have had more success than you could possibly
have imagined.* —John Ruskin

*We don't look at the trouble we see right now, we look
beyond them to what God is doing in our lives*
(2 Corinthians 4:18 ELT).

IT feels strange to think about it…to put it into
words…to say it. I just lost my job. I've been home
all day on Thursday—and it's not even Thanksgiving!
I'm still not sure it's even beginning to sink in yet, but
it's getting there.

I was a financial planner,…I got paid based on a
percentage of the assets I managed for clients. I wasn't
the only employee to be laid off. Two others were laid
off as well, and that's pretty significant when you realize
they only have a staff of ten.

Honestly I didn't get upset, angry, bitter or nasty when

the bosses told me I was getting laid off. I was a little shocked, but I am a financial planner—I deal with the future. At first I wanted to laugh, as if it were some kind of a joke. But I quickly felt my stomach wrenching and I started thinking, *What do I do now?*

I thanked my boss for giving me the opportunity to work with them for a year and made my way back to my office to pack up my things.

Just as fears started consuming my mind, I remembered to pray. I didn't have a fancy prayer, and I didn't use a lot of words. I just thanked God for all the blessings He had already given me, and I submitted to His will. I know that God has a plan for my life, and I know it's better than anything I've tried thinking up on my own. In that moment, I truly handed my worries over to God, I felt the crushing fear lift from my heart, and God's peace took its place. I didn't feel like crying anymore. I didn't need to. God was in control—and He still is today.[1]

ACCEPT WHAT HAS HAPPENED

Don't go through the denial phase that it didn't happen or even "it shouldn't have happened." Don't go there. There's no healing in constantly reminding yourself of "what *should* have happened."

Sometimes it's very hard to accept that you've been "kicked out on the streets," or you've been "cut." They sent you "packing," or you've been "fired." You can't change what has happened, so deal with it!

Sometimes companies have to downsize because of bottom-line income. Sometimes companies have to change their futures, and you are not in their plans. There may be many good reasons why you were "cut loose," so accept it.

Tell yourself, "I'm not going to complain about my company, nor am I going to blame anyone—I'm going to move on."

Honestly, that can be hard to do because of your hurt, embarrassment, or financial problems. You will get healthy when you make up your mind that you will find another job, that you will consciously pursue another job, and give all your energies to the future.

Lord, forgive me when I hang on to the past when the future has been radically changed. Help me deal with life's blows, even when I don't want to face the future. Give me a realistic view of the past, and help me plan for the future. Amen.

Controlling Your Emotions

After you leave your "former" place of employment, you will be faced with many active feelings. You have suddenly lost your livelihood, and it hits you in the ego and pocketbook, and most of all, in your self-esteem. You are likely to face a junction of emotions— shame, anger, confusion, panic, and sometimes self-blame. You blame yourself for losing the job when you shouldn't do that.

You need to control your feelings and look at this through God's eyes. Yes, God is in control, and He wants to teach you something through this experience. Yes, you can get a new job and it may be a better one. Yes, you need to stay positive and not give in to your negative emotions. Why re-hash what happened when you were informed that your job was terminated? It's time to move on, so get ready to move.

Lord, make me realistic in all of life's problems. Help me see things the way they are. Help me make realistic plans about the future. Amen.

Find Out Your Benefits

You can determine most of your benefits by talking to someone in the Human Resources department before leaving the company. Ask the following and other such questions:

1. What is my severance pay?

2. What will happen to my health insurance?

3. How long will my 401k be carried?

4. Do I have vacation time or sick days coming for which I can be paid?

5. Are there any other resources or services that the Human Resources department offers you, i.e., do they have job re-training, job referral services, or counseling available for those who have been terminated?

Know Your Rights

If you live in the United States, you have certain rights regarding employment, and you ought to know them. Check the contract you may have with your company. Were you wrongfully dismissed due to age, disability, pregnancy, or race? What about collective bargaining agreements? Also, remember that union workers have a vast number of rights available to them that are not available to non-union workers. If you feel that you were wrongfully dismissed, and you want to consider legal actions, remember there may be costs involved in contacting a lawyer. On the other hand, there may be costs involved if you don't contact a lawyer.

Ask About References

Like it or not, you will have to do some "damage control" when you are terminated. Talk with your supervisor and minimize the fact that he had to terminate you. Tell him you want to get on with a job search and ask him what will be his attitude for prospective employers if they were to call for a reference about you.

If you create a negative confrontation with your former employer, you will not get any help from him or her with your next job. Also, he or she won't say anything to you for fear of being sued—remember, we live in a litmus society.

But because of our litmus society, your former supervisor will often go to great pains to smooth the exit for you. Your boss wants you to leave on reasonably good terms, and most likely will give you an acceptable reference if you can calmly discuss your exit and new job; this may be a good "teachable" experience for you. Perhaps you'll learn something in this conversation that will help you in the next job.

FILE FOR UNEMPLOYMENT

One of the first things you should do is to get your unemployment compensation application into the state unemployment office as soon as possible. The sooner you have your application in, the sooner you will get that first check. Remember, it may not arrive until two weeks to one month.

CHECK HEALTH INSURANCE

Check on your health insurance. If your company has 20 or more employees, they must legally offer health insurance coverage through COBRA (Consolidated Omnibus Budget Reconciliation Act of 1986) to terminated employees for 18 months. Most of the time, you will have to pay the full premiums, but if you are going to keep the self-coverage, this is one way to get it done.

YOUR RÉSUMÉ

When we talk about a résumé, it is a document that summarizes your relevant job experiences, qualifications, and education; it is usually prepared to send to a prospective employer to get an interview when seeking employment.

Remember, your next supervisor has probably received many résumés, and he or she only scans them. Your supervisor may not read your résumé carefully, until ready to make a decision on hiring someone for the job. Therefore, write your résumé for someone who is *scanning your résumé.*

If the résumé is too long, it probably won't be read. If it's too short, it probably doesn't have enough information. Remember, your résumé is the first thing that your potential supervisor reads when determining if you will be invited for an interview. Therefore, your résumé is perhaps the most important "marketing" tool you have to share with everyone looking for a worker with your abilities.

Your résumé must include your work history, and it must come across clearly that you have the credentials to be successful in the new job. Therefore, prepare your résumé because you believe in yourself, so you can get your next supervisor to believe in you. The key word is *credibility*. When they read your résumé, they must believe that you can do the job for which they are searching.

When you write your résumé, don't volunteer that you were terminated at your previous place of employment. Those who interview you will probably ask because of the very fact that you are no longer working there. If asked, remember a couple of things:

1. Don't play the "blame game" and put all the blame on your former employer for firing you. If you do, the person interviewing you will realize that you will blame him and your next job also.

2. Do not say anything negative about your former employer.

MAKE A BUDGET

One of the first things to do when you're terminated is to take stock of your situation. "Take stock" means looking at your available finances for the next few months. How much money do you have to support you—and your family—before you get another job? Involve your spouse in this process if you are married.

You should have a budget already in place, so go through your budget line by line and mark the items that are absolute necessities. That means dining out and entertainment has to go. Then look at all the contracts you have signed—satellite television, rent, garbage collection, utilities, heating, insurance, gasoline, land-based phone, cell phone, etc. What can be eliminated?

Calculate how much your absolute monthly expenses will be.

Verify how much money you have in savings. This involves emergency funds as well as other money that's been put away for a rainy day. Determine how long your existing money will last before you get a new job—six months, one year, two years. (This is why you should have an emergency fund.)

Make phone calls to reduce some of the essential bills. This means cutting all of the extras on your phone, negotiate to get out of your television network contract, put insurance on a six-month payment plan, check on short-term health insurance.

If at all possible, do everything you can to not dive into your retirement funds.

Plan Tomorrow

Make a plan for tomorrow. The worst thing is to wake up tomorrow and not know what to do on the day after you get fired. Make a "to do" list of contacts concerning a new job that you will make tomorrow. Write out a complete schedule of all the things you'll do on the day after getting released.

THANKS

Write a letter of appreciation to your former boss; and if you have more than one supervisor, write to each telling them how much you appreciated working there. Even if you're mad or hurt, do it anyway. It'll be good therapy for you. Request a letter of reference from them. That may be necessary at the next place to explain why you were released.

DEVELOP A PATH OF ACTION

You are on a quest to find a job. It's like taking a trip. And what do you do when taking a trip? You plan how to get there, how to travel, and you usually make some provisions for any problems you'll encounter on the way.

Approach job hunting like planning a trip. There is a destination, so map out a path to get there. Then plan what you're going to do along the path. Consider your options, your assets, and always keep a strong, positive determination to find your "destination."

You have to do more than just think about the job you want. Write down some random thoughts about the job you want, and then arrange your ideas into a visual goal. You might even make a list of the ten best places you'd like to work. Then make a list of the ten best jobs at that place you would like to do.

Suppose your thinking comes up short. Think back to your past job and look at the various jobs up the ladder ahead of you, the jobs that paid more money or more prestige. What would it have taken you to get those jobs, and why did you not get them? These considerations will help you choose the next job that is best for you.

Market Yourself

Whether you like it or not, now that you are looking for a job, you will have to market yourself to everyone; not just your potential employer. You have to market yourself to friends so they can help you "plug" into a job. You have to market yourself to all your contacts because they may know about an open position. Then you must market yourself to every potential employer. You must project an image, just as in marketing a product. Know what type of image you want to project to your various public. Remember, people want an optimistic, energetic person who is excited about the future. They'll want somebody who is willing to work and has the qualifications to get the job done for them.

Market Your Network

Within a day of being terminated, contact everyone you know and let them know you are in the market for a new job. Forget embarrassment, your call or letter to them must be positive and upbeat; as if you were applying for a job. Let all your contacts know what a good employee you would be for a new company.

Whatever you do, don't focus on why your previous company was wrong to fire you, or the problem you had with your boss, or any of the other problems you may want to ventilate. Keep your contact positive and think about the future. Let them know what you're interested in doing and what value you can add to a company. You never know what resources your contacts have. One of these contacts may have the right job for you.

BE PREPARED FOR DISAPPOINTMENTS

As you market yourself, be prepared for "near misses." There are going to be some jobs that you almost get; as a matter of fact, you may be one of the last two candidates chosen, but the other guy or gal gets it. You can't live in the past, so don't blame yourself for not getting that job. If the other person got the job, he or she was probably better qualified in the eyes of the interviewer; though not necessarily the best person for the job.

Yes, you will be frustrated on your job-seeking pilgrimage; but always keep your final destination in mind. Yes, you are looking for a job; and yes, you will find one.

So keep marketing, keep moving, keep branching out. Those without a job have a tendency to stay home. Don't give in to housework, nor should you spend your time running errands with your spouse. Get out there where the jobs are, stay on the computer and work the Internet. Expand your networking, keep your energy high, and stay active in smart ways. Everything you do must be focused on getting a job.

Lord, there will be disappointments in life, prepare me for them. When I'm "blindsided" by failure, help me learn the lesson You have for me. Help me be strong not to make that mistake again. Keep me positive. Amen.

JOB SEARCH IS A FULL-TIME JOB

Like it or not, a job search is a full-time job. Just as you gave eight or more hours a day at your previous job, you must now spend at least eight hours a day to find that next job. And don't forget overtime, just as you receive extra compensation for working overtime, you may get that job by continuing to work on your computer late into the afternoon or early evening. And if worry has you sleepless, get up and go to the computer and start searching.

TARGET AND FOCUS

Very seldom will employers come looking for you; you must go looking for them. If they don't know you exist, obviously they'll never offer you a job. Even if they have a stack of résumés on a desk, it doesn't mean you'll get the job. Remember a basic principle: *you will choose where you will work.* Therefore, determine the kind and size of company you want to work for and the type of work you want to do. You can even choose the type of supervisor you'd like to have, as well as the place you want to work (most of the time).

Therefore, looking for a job is not like shooting a shot gun, scattering the shots over a wide target. No! Looking for a job should be like shooting a rifle. Focus on the target, and bring all your energies to bear on the job that you want.

THOROUGHLY RESEARCH RESOURCES

When you begin looking for a new job, there are many places where potential jobs are located. You need to know where they are, then go search for the one you want.

Your local library will have magazines, journals, and information on where jobs are available. Ask your librarian about "source books" for the various industries and where you can find as much information as possible on an industry, similar to your ideal "job type." You'll be amazed at what you can find in a library.

HEAD HUNTERS

These are recruiters who are looking for recruits for available jobs and they get a percentage of your income for connecting you to a job. Like any other occupation, there are good head hunters and there are dead ends.

Head hunters are also called recruiters or employment agencies. Some of them are excellent at "searching" for the right person, and connecting the right person to the right job. But most of them can't help you unless your qualifications match up with their client's requirements.

Where do you find a recruiter? You will find them online, from your librarian, or Google is a good place to find almost anything.

Internet Job Sites

On the Internet you will find several employment job sites such as Monster.com, CareerBuilder.com, Dice.com, and hotjobs.yahoo.com. Obviously, a job site is a business, so you're going to have to pay for any help they give you. Some want you to pay up front, and then not help you. Others will take a percentage of your new income after you are employed.

These job sites can "eat up" much of your valuable time, so use the search tools to match your needs to a job. Again, Google can help you find them.

Target Job Opportunities

Make a list of companies where you would like to work. But make sure these are companies that are now hiring. If a company has laid off many people, it would not be smart to spend much energy there. Rather, look for companies that have a solid balance sheet, and look for companies that are expanding.

Then identify the person in each company who could be your next supervisor. These are the people to whom you're going to send an email, letting them know of your interest. Remember to attach a résumé.

Getting a job is similar to catching a fish, the more hooks you have in the water, the more likely you are to catch one fish, or more than one fish. So don't send an email to just one place. Put a lot of hooks in the water.

Your email should let the person know why you want to work there and what value you bring to the company.

Focus on What You Can Control, Not on Things You Can't Control

When you first heard that you were being terminated, perhaps the worst scenarios went through your mind. You began to think bankruptcy, loss of reputation, loss of valuable things (house, car, or even marriage). It's only human to reach for the "panic button," but don't do it.

There are many things in life that you cannot control, and losing a job apparently is one of those. You can't control what happens *to* you, but you can control what happens *in* you. You can control the way you're going to respond to your problems. You can control what you do tomorrow, you can control how you write your résumé, you can control how many job contacts you'll make each day.

Look Again at Your Faith

You may have heard a sermon on "Jehovah Jirah," which means *"the Lord Will Provide"* (Gen. 22:14). This means God will take care of you, even though you don't know how He will do it, where you will work, or maybe even where your next meal may come from. But you have the promise of God that He will take care of you. If you believe "God has a plan for your life," then you realize that you are in excellent hands, for God knows all the details of the future.

So what must you do? Put God first in your job search, even before finances, security, or prestige. Ask the question: "Lord, *where* do You want me to work?" And you might ask a second question: "Lord, *what* do You want me to do for You in the next job?"

When you put God first in your life, you agree with the words of Jesus: *"But seek first the kingdom of God and His righteousness, and all these things shall be added to you"* (Matt. 6:33).

Why did Jesus say to first seek God's Kingdom? Because He knew the fleshly desires of His children. Jesus said:

> *Do not lay up for yourselves treasures on earth, where moth and rust destroy and where thieves break in and steal; but lay up for yourselves treasures in heaven.... For where your treasure is, there your heart will be also* (Matthew 6:19-21).

Make Sure Your Christian Discipline Is in Place

Christian discipline involves the study of the Scriptures each day so that you allow God to speak to you. Then you're going to pray to God each day. This is when you talk to Him about your next job. Keep a two-way conversation going between the Lord and you, so He can guide you to the next job.

> *Lord, I will pray daily and I will pray throughout each day. I will continue praying until I get the answer I seek. I will read and study Your Word to find Your will for my life. Speak to me through the Scriptures. Amen.*

Don't Give in to Your Fears or Anxieties

Remember, Paul told us: *"Do not lose heart. Even though our outward man is perishing, yet the inward man is being renewed day by day"* (2 Cor. 4:16).

Accept God's Will

The Lord has promised to be with us in every aspect of our lives, so that includes a job search. It's not enough to just pray and ask God to lead you "magically" to some job that's out there. God will not violate the laws of communication by "dropping" a perfect job in your lap. God is interested in both the means and the end result. God expects you to talk to many people, and use the avenues of communication to locate a job. In that process, God can lead you through small details to help find that job. While the world says, "The devil is in the details," you must believe that God is the details.

The Lord promised: *"I will instruct you and teach you in the way you should go; I will guide you with My eye"* (Ps. 32:8).

This means that God will help in little ways to uncover facts, insights, or even contacts of how to find a job. By faith you must look in every place to learn all you can about a job. It's out there waiting for you.

The opposite of faith is doubt. And doubt's brother is fear. When we begin to doubt God, we fear for the future. And both doubt and fear have a long-lost cousin that you don't need to entertain—despair and anxiety. When despair takes over, we give up, refuse to be proactive, and we give into our worst nightmares—joblessness, bankruptcy, humiliation, and starvation.

So how does doubt worm its way into our thinking? Usually when we begin asking questions of God. We ask, "God, why did You let me get fired?" as though it's His will that this calamity has happened to us. And then we ask the second question: "God, why now?" We want to know why God allowed your firing to happen at this specific time period. Because all of us have many plans in life, you may get terminated when you have a big anniversary coming up, or you were in the process of buying a new house, or you were in the process of financially taking care of a problem.

There's no such thing as a coincidence in life, we Christians believe that *"all things work together for good"* (Rom. 8:28). Therefore, nothing just randomly happens to the children of God. The root meaning of the word *coincidence* is *coincide*, which means two sides meet precisely. Therefore, there are no coincidences in God's plan; He brings two sides together to perfectly match the need of the moment.

Look back and review all the different ways God has worked in your life. Think about the question "Why, God?" and understand that God has opened many doors in your life, and your firing may not be a closed door, but your termination can be an open door.

When you think of the question, "Why now?," remember God's timing is always perfect, even though you don't understand it. Look back at all the ways God's timing has worked in the past. That will help you understand the future.

Lord, I don't understand why calamities come in my life, but I accept them and I will work hard to overcome my misfortune. Guide me as I study my problems so I'll know how to solve them. Give me the ability to climb out of this ditch and get back to my normal life. Help me take the right steps and make the right contacts to solve my problem. Give me courage and faith in this problem to solve it and live for You. Amen.

QUESTIONS FOR THOUGHT

1. How can a person accept employment release as a Christian and keep his or her testimony strong for Christ?

2. How or what can a person say to his or her supervisor while being released?

3. How or what can a person do in relationship to the company after being released?

4. What should a person do the first day after being released?

5. What should a person look for in the next job that will keep the person from being released again?

6. How can a person take inventory of himself or herself after being released to make sure it doesn't happen in the next job?

7. What should people learn about "God's plan" for their lives after they are released from their job?

8. What should be a Christian's attitude during release and the search for a new job?

ENDNOTE

1. See Cracker Jack Greenback, "Laid Off—Day One: Pray, Relax, and Take Stock," available at http://www. crackerjackgreenback.com/goals/laid-off-day-one-pray-relax-and-take-stock (accessed November 18, 2009).

Chapter 4

Realize Your Job Is a Gift From God!

Dave Earley

Work while you have the light. You are responsible for the
talent that has been entrusted to you.
—Henri Frederic Amiel

Your work matters to God.[1]

WORK IS MORE THAN A FOUR-LETTER WORD

MOST of us will spend a large percentage of the best waking hours of our adult lives at our job. Therefore, what we believe about work is extremely important. If we do not have a right understanding of work, we cannot live a complete and successful Christian life. If we do not have an accurate view of work, we will be unfulfilled in work and in life. If we do not see work as God sees it, we cannot really walk in close fellowship with God.

Unfortunately, most of us have a messed-up view of work. We tend to view work as a burden to get rid of as soon as possible. Or we wrongly assume that work is a god that will bring us ultimate fulfillment. Neither is true. We think that God is only interested in what we do on Sundays and not what happens between the hours of nine to five, Monday through Friday—which is also untrue. For some, work becomes a spiritual stumbling block as we get lost in the quest for more money, more power, and more prestige. For others, work becomes a minefield of dangerous ethical and moral issues. They mistakenly believe that they have to leave their soul at the door when they walk into their place of employment.

Before we can pray rightly about our job, we need to have a biblically accurate view of our work. We must clearly understand that:

+ Work is more than a four-letter word!

+ Work is a gift from God.

+ Work is not beneath the dignity of God.

+ Work is not something we do apart from God.

+ Work is not something that should be allowed to take the place of God.

+ Work is more than merely a platform from which we can evangelize.

+ Work is valuable in itself.

+ Work must be done with the attitude of doing our best for God and for His glory.

Lord, open my eyes to see my work as You see it. Thank You for my employment. May I do my very best each day on the job. Transform my attitude toward my job. I will work every day as though I'm working for You. Amen.

GOD CREATED WORK TO BE MEANINGFUL

As mentioned in the Introduction, God's first appearance in the Bible is not that of Savior, Shepherd, Prophet, Priest, or King. No. God reveals Himself to us first as a Worker! Maybe you never thought of it this way, but God greatly dignified work by being a worker. *"In the beginning God created the heavens and the earth"* (Gen. 1:1).

*And on the seventh day God ended His **work** which He had done, and He rested on the seventh day from all His **work** which He had done. Then God blessed the seventh day and sanctified it, because in it He rested from all His **work** which God had created and made* (Genesis 2:2-3).

Not only did God work in the past, but He is still at work today. He is continuing to uphold, sustain, and maintain the amazing, immense, and expanding universe He created.

For by Him all things were created that are in heaven and that are on earth, visible and invisible, whether thrones or dominions or principalities or powers. All things were created through Him and for Him. And He is before all things, and in Him all things consist. And He is the head of the body, the church, who is the beginning, the firstborn from the dead, that in all things He may have the preeminence (Colossians 1:16-18).

This very moment God is actively at work redeeming, reconciling, and restoring fallen humankind to a right relationship with

Himself and others. Jesus is now at work preparing an incredible place for us.

> *In My Father's house are many mansions; if it were not so, I would have told you. I go to prepare a place for you. And if I go and prepare a place for you...* (John 14:2-3).

Work is more than a necessary evil. It is more than a four-letter word. It is a gift from God. It is honorable, meaningful, and important, because God is the ultimate Worker.

> *The **works** of the Lord are great, studied by all who have pleasure in them. His **work** is honorable and glorious, and His righteousness endures forever* (Psalm 111:2-3).

When my boys were little they all went through a phase when they wanted to be like Dad and work with Dad. When I would mow the lawn, my oldest son, Daniel, would follow behind me with his plastic toy mower. When I would get up to go to work, my middle son, Andrew, would put on my shoes and glasses, grab my briefcase, and try to jump in the car to go with me. It is natural for children to want to work with their parents.

Researchers tell us that children of this generation struggle greatly with self-esteem issues. One reason is that there is not much work for them to accomplish. Too often parents do not give them chores to do. Instead of helping milk the cows or bring in the harvest as in previous eras, children are sitting in front of the television or a video game. Healthy self-esteem is not developed in children because healthy work is not being accomplished by them.

But the Bible is clear. From the beginning, God's intent was to partner with us by working together in the lush paradise of the Garden of Eden. God instilled and infused work with dignity because He invited us to work with Him.

> *The Lord God planted a garden eastward in Eden, and there He put the man whom He had formed. … Then the Lord God took the man and put him in the garden of Eden to tend and keep it* (Genesis 2:8-15).

Work is God's gift to us. It is His provision for us in a number of ways:

1. Through work we can serve people (see Gal. 5:13).

2. Through work we meet our own needs (see 2 Thess. 3:10).

3. Through work we meet our family's needs (see 1 Tim. 5:8).

4. Through work we earn money to give to others (see Lev. 19:10; Eph. 4:28).

Work is meaningful and important. Work is a gift from God. Just as you matter to God, your work matters to God.

> *Lord, forgive me when I haven't been serious about my job, and forgive me when I haven't done my best. I want my job to be valuable to me. Give me seriousness about my work and make it meaningful to me. Amen.*

SIN-TAINTED WORK

In Genesis chapter 1, we read of God creating the universe. In chapter 2 we read of God inviting man to work. Everything was going so well, but in chapter 3 we read of man choosing to disobey God and of being forced to accept the consequences for his sin. First man was separated from God because of his sin. As a result, he experienced fear, guilt, shame, and ultimately death.

The second result of sin was that the earth was cursed.

Then to Adam He said, "Because you have heeded the voice of your wife, and have eaten from the tree of which I commanded you, saying, 'You shall not eat of it': cursed is the ground for your sake; in toil you shall eat of it all the days of your life. Both thorns and thistles it shall bring forth for you, and you shall eat the herb of the field. In the sweat of your face you shall eat bread till you return to the ground, for out of it you were taken; for dust you are, and to dust you shall return" (Genesis 3:17-19).

Notice carefully that sin and the resulting curse did not result in "having to work." Work existed *before* sin and *before* the curse. The curse did not create work. It simply made work more difficult and frustrating. The curse was placed on the ground, not on work. After man's fall into sin, the lush garden developed weeds. Droughts, floods, devastating weather, and devouring insects were introduced to the earth. From this point on, it became much more difficult to produce a crop, to raise an animal, to make a living. But the Bible is very clear—while the environment of work was cursed, the work was not cursed.

Make no mistake about it. A much worse curse would be to have no work to do. Go to an urban area where the majority of the population does not work, but rather lives on government assistance. People without jobs feel less significant. They take less pride in their appearance and in their property. They get involved in more addictive behaviors and participate in more crime.

The third result of sin was that work and workers became inherently imperfect. As a result, we must work among people who are sinful. *"As it is written: 'There is none righteous, no, not one'"* (Rom. 3:10).

The fourth result of sin was that we now work in settings that are imperfect. Since the fall into sin and the resulting curse, all of creation is groaning under the weight of futility and corruption.

For the creation was subjected to futility, not willingly, but because of Him who subjected it in hope; because the creation itself also will be delivered from the bondage of corruption into the glorious liberty of the children of God. For we know that the whole creation groans and labors with birth pangs together until now (Romans 8:20-22).

When sin came, a certain futility was introduced to earthly work, even successful work. Probably no one expressed this better than Solomon. His first few years as king of Israel were a blur of activity. His achievements were prolific and colossal.

I made my works great, I built myself houses, and planted myself vineyards. I made myself gardens and orchards, and I planted all kinds of fruit trees in them. I made myself water pools from which to water the growing trees of the grove. I acquired male and female servants, and had servants born in my house. Yes, I had greater possessions of herds and flocks than all who were in Jerusalem before me. I also gathered for myself silver and gold and the special treasures of kings and of the provinces. I acquired male and female singers, the delights of the sons of men, and musical instruments of all kinds. So I became great and excelled more than all who were before me in Jerusalem. Also my wisdom remained with me. Whatever my eyes desired I did not keep from them. I did not withhold my heart from any pleasure, for my heart rejoiced in all my labor; and this was my reward from all my labor (Ecclesiastes 2:4-10).

After devoting himself so wholeheartedly to his accomplishments, Solomon expected to be fulfilled and content. But notice carefully how a life of work without God left him feeling.

*Then I looked on all the works that my hands had done and on the labor in which I had toiled; and indeed **all was vanity and grasping for the wind.** There was **no profit** under the sun* (Ecclesiastes 2:11).

Note the futility expressed by Solomon's words—*"all was vanity," "grasping for the wind," "no profit."* Earthly work has been stained by futility. If you wash the dishes, they will just get dirty again. If you cure one disease, another breaks out. Because of the curse of sin, our work may feel as though it has no lasting importance.

But cheer up, there is good news:

Lord, I confess my sin and my failings. Forgive me when I've not done my best, and forgive me for every mistake on the job. Cleanse my sin by the blood of Christ and help me live above my sins, and help me work above my weaknesses and past failures. Amen.

CHRIST RETURNED MEANING TO WORK

Sin has made the working world a jungle. But fear not. Jesus is the Lion of the tribe of Judah and King of the jungle! Just as God the Father birthed work with dignity, Jesus returns honor to work.

Work is not our enemy—sin is. Jesus dealt a death blow to sin that can be realized individually when we give our lives to Him and will be experienced globally at His second coming. We can do much better than merely survive our jobs. We can *thrive* in our jobs.

What then shall we say to these things? If God is for us, who can be against us? He who did not spare His own Son, but delivered Him up for us all, how shall He not with Him also freely give us all things? Who shall bring a charge against God's elect? It is God who justifies. Who is he who condemns? It is Christ who died, and furthermore is also risen, who is even at the right hand of God, who also makes intercession for us? Who shall separate us from the love of Christ? Shall tribulation, or distress, or persecution, or famine, or nakedness, or peril, or sword? As it is written: "For Your sake we are killed all day long; we are accounted as sheep for the slaughter." Yet in all these things we are more than conquerors through Him who loved us (Romans 8:31-37).

God birthed work with value and meaning. Jesus can rebirth your work with honor and purpose. How? By your determination to do all of your work as unto God. Why? To bring Him glory, the glory He deserves, and to receive His commendation for a job well done.

Bondservants, obey in all things your masters according to the flesh, not with eye-service, as men-pleasers, but in sincerity of heart, fearing God. And whatever you do, do it heartily, as to the Lord and not to men, knowing that from the Lord you will receive the reward of the inheritance; for you serve the Lord Christ (Colossians 3:22-24).

Paul told the Colossian believers to be good workers, even if they had lousy bosses. They were to work with good attitudes and genuine, sincere hearts. They were to do their absolute best. They were to take their work seriously, realizing that ultimately God was their boss and that He notes their actions and attitudes. They were also to stay confident, and eventually the Lord would reward their efforts.

How to Pray for Your Job

Lord, I thank God for the gift of work. I acknowledge that You were the first and greatest Worker. May I be like You—a good worker. Please give me the right attitude about my work in general, and my job in particular. Help me get up every morning with the view of using my job as another opportunity to bring glory to You. Help me realize that You are my ultimate Boss and You take my attitudes and actions about work very seriously. Remind me that eventually You will reward my good and honorable work. Amen.

Questions for Thought

1. Why do some people—including Christians—have a sour attitude about their job?

2. What are some Christian attitudes that will make a person's job more enjoyable, productive, and efficient?

3. What can a person do to make his or her job more meaningful?

4. What can a person do when "stuck" in a job that's degrading, dull, and unexciting?

5. What is the relationship between sin and a person's job? How does sin destroy someone's effectiveness, enjoyment, or even continuance on the job?

6. How can people change their attitude when they hate their job, don't do their best, and would like to quit?

Endnote

1. Doug Sherman and William Hendricks, *Your Work Matters to God* (Colorado Springs, CO: NavPress, 1987).

Section II

Your Long-range View

Chapter 5

Your Job Is Your Ministry—Pray for Yourself as a Christian Worker

Dave Earley

Blessed is he who has found his work; let him ask no other blessedness. —Leo Buscaglia

Work becomes worship when you dedicate it to God and perform it with an awareness of his presence.[1]

IN *Safely Home*, his fictional story of Li Quan, the persecuted Chinese Christian, Randy Alcorn does a wonderful job of showing us what it is to work for Jesus, no matter how menial the task.

Li Quan's father was a talented man who was forced to serve as a street cleaner because of persecution. His father brought respect and dignity to a demeaning job by striving to do his best as unto the Lord.

Li Quan was a brilliant Chinese professor. Yet because of persecution in China, he found himself working as a humble key maker. Like his father, he brought honor to his work by giving his best to the Lord.

Later he was forced to go to prison because of his faith. There he was locked in isolation and had no way to contact the other prisoners. Alcorn shares:

The guard peered into Quan's cell through the little, barred window, which was two handbreadths across... Quan could see the contempt in his eyes.

"Stop smiling!" he yelled.

"I am not smiling," Quan said.

"Yes, you are!" shouted the guard.

...Suddenly, Quan stood and pressed his face against the bars. "Guard!" Quan called. When he didn't come, he called louder. "Su Gan!"

The guard came back and rattled the door violently. "Who told you my name? Be silent or I will come in and make you silent!"

"Su Gan, sir, please, I have a request for you."

"Unless you can pay me, I care nothing for your requests."

"Can I do some labor for you?"

Quan saw in the jailer's eyes surprise mixed with contempt.

"This prison is so filthy," Quan said. "There is waste everywhere. The rats and roaches feed on it...Quan can help you. Let me go into the cells one by one and clean up this filthy place. Give me water and a brush and soap, and I will show you what I can do!"[2]

Quan offered to serve the jailer and the other prisoners by disposing of human waste from the filthy jail cells. He would try to scrub each cell until it was spotless, all as a testimony for Christ.

After several months, his American friend came to visit him in prison. Alcorn continues:

> Ben stood in the chilly winter air. As usual, he waited nervously, trying to keep warm and to will Quan out of the black hole. Someone was being led out of the building now, a frail, older man with a pronounced limp and yellow skin, as if he had jaundice or hepatitis.
>
> …He felt his heart freeze. "Quan?" He tried to disguise his horror. They touched right index fingers through the fence. "You smell like…soap."
>
> "Yes." Quan beamed, his face and voice surprisingly animated. "This is better than I smelled last time, yes? I have wonderful news! You must tell my family and house church. God has answered prayer. He has given me a ministry!"
>
> "What?"
>
> "I go from cell to cell, bringing Yesu's message."
>
> "But I thought you were in an isolated cell."
>
> "God opened the door. I go to the other men. Most have never had anyone else come into their cell except to beat them. I help and serve them as I clean their cells. I bring them the love of Yesu. Twelve men I have visited. When I left their cells, six I did not leave alone."
>
> "What do you mean?"
>
> "When I left, Yesu was with them. Three were already believers, one of them a pastor…. Three more bowed

their knees to Yesu, who promises never to leave or forsake them…I will teach as I wash."

"The guards let you do this?"

"The smell that used to cling to the guards is now almost gone. Their shoes are not ruined. The prisoners are excited…to realize that even if they die here, they will have eternal life."[3]

Sounds more like a revival meeting than a prison.

Lord, teach me to work diligently in every situation, as did Quan. Help me overcome every stressful predicament I find in life. Use my work to change the people I work with and I work for. Amen.

Your Job Is Your Ministry

All of us who are Christians are *Christian* workers, or at least we should be. Whether we are receiving a salary, punching a time clock, or volunteering at a homeless shelter, we should view and fulfill all of our responsibilities in the manner of Christ-followers. Our work today may be doing housework, homeschooling our children, or cleaning up the yard. Whether it is something we are getting paid for or something we are not being paid for, all of our work is endued with meaning, purpose, and honor when we do it for Christ.

Let's walk through several key verses that illumine and inform our responsibilities as Christian workers. Following these biblical commands allow us to turn any job into a ministry. Understanding these verses can help inspire us as we pray for ourselves as Christian workers.

Obey and Respect Your Bosses

Bondservants, obey in all things your masters according to the flesh, not with eye-service, as men-pleasers, but in sincerity of heart, fearing God (Colossians 3:22).

In too many work settings, the employees work hard only as long as the boss is watching them. But when the boss turns his or her back, the employees waste time surfing the Internet, tending to personal matters, or in frivolous conversations with one another. Yet Paul is clear with the Colossians. Christian workers are to submit to their bosses and obey their superiors' wishes, even when their bosses are not looking.

In the typical work setting, everything seems good on the surface. But under the surface, when the boss is out of sight, there is often an ugly hostility toward the person in authority. Employees backbite, ridicule, complain, slander, mock, and speak disrespectfully of the one in authority—and that is the response of some *paid* employees. Imagine how slaves must have responded to their masters in the first century!

Yet Paul is very clear, Christian workers need to go to work every day with a great attitude toward their bosses. We are to obey and respect our bosses even when they are out of sight. The word Paul uses for "obey" is a compound word crudely rendered "to listen under."[4] It means to be actively under the authority of another. In other words, we need to do our best work with our best attitudes.

But you say, "I have a good attitude and am respectful most of the time, regarding most of the things they ask of me." That's not good enough. Paul said that we are to *obey in **all** things.*

But you say, "You don't know my boss!" "He (or she) is an arrogant pain in the neck." Or, "They are totally incompetent." All of which may be true, but that's not the point. We do not respect authority because authority is respectable, but because they are in authority over us. God placed them into that role of authority and God is our ultimate authority. We must submit to the position, even if we find it difficult to submit to the person in the position.

Although in Romans 13 Paul is directly addressing the issue of respecting governmental authorities, the principles apply to our relationships with all of our earthly authorities. We are commanded to respect them, including our bosses. They have been placed there by God. To resist, disrespect, or disobey them is to resist God.

Let every soul be subject to the governing authorities. For there is no authority except from God, and the authorities that exist are appointed by God. Therefore whoever resists the authority resists the ordinance of God, and those who resist will bring judgment on themselves (Romans 13:1-2).

But you say, "How far does obeying my boss go?" Good question. My answer is that you obey as long as what he or she is asking you to do is not illegal, immoral, unethical, or clearly anti-God. If you are asked to do something illegal, immoral, unethical, or anti-God, you can take the matter up with a higher authority or find another place of employment.

Do Your Best

*And whatever you do, **do it heartily**, as to the Lord and not to men* (Colossians 3:23).

We are to go to work with the intention of working. This seems obvious, but too many workers want a paycheck without doing much work. When I was in high school, I had a friend who accepted a summer job with the city work crew. He was so excited to get to spend an entire summer working alongside seasoned workers. After the first week, I asked him how it was going. "Terrible," he said. "Instead of doing all we can, they spend all day trying to figure out how to do as little as possible. When I try to work hard, the other workers yell at me to take it easy or I'll make them look bad. It has taken us a week to do the equivalent of one honest day's work. I hate it."

When speaking of work, Paul tells us to *"do it."* The word used here means "to work, to work at it, to do business, to produce, to exercise, to earn."[5] The real satisfaction from work does not come from avoiding it, but "doing it"—and doing it well.

Regarding work, Paul told us not only *what* to do—*"do it,"* but also *how* to do it—*"do it heartily."* The word *heartily* is the Greek term for "soul" (*psyche*). A crude translation would be "work from out of your soul" or "as you work, put your soul into it."[6]

Do It for Jesus

And whatever you do, do it heartily, **as to the Lord** *and not to men* (Colossians 3:23).

We are to work *"as to the Lord."* In the big picture, when we go to work "we serve Christ."

For the Christ-follower, work is another opportunity to worship. When we work, we are to do it for Jesus. Human bosses are faulty and frustrating. But ultimately, they are not who we are working for. We are to work for the Lord. This attitude transforms any job into a ministry unto the Lord.

Yes, we are to work hard and heartily for our human bosses, just *as if* we were working for the Lord, because ultimately we are. Our work is bigger than our boss, and our paycheck—it is ultimately about Jesus and eternal rewards.

Christian employees should be able to offer every day's effort up to the Lord as an offering. We should bring a reverence to our jobs. Going to work should simply be another opportunity to worship.

Work for the Real Rewards

And whatever you do, do it heartily, as to the Lord and not to men, knowing that from the Lord you will **receive the reward** *of the inheritance; for you serve the Lord Christ* (Colossians 3:23-24).

There are many great rewards that come to us when we work hard and heartily as unto the Lord:

1. Prosperity:

The soul of a lazy man desires, and has nothing; but the soul of the diligent shall be made rich (Proverbs 13:4).

2. Recognition: Excellent work is almost always recognized and rewarded by others. Solomon wrote:

Do you see a man who excels in his work? He will stand before kings; he will not stand before unknown men (Proverbs 22:29).

In other words, excellent workers will be noticed and admired. They will always end up in demand. They don't have to take a backseat to anyone.

3. Commendation: For those first-century slaves, the rewards they worked for would not be experienced until they were with Jesus. Then they could enjoy His words of commendation and His offer of greater responsibility and authority in His Kingdom.

So he who had received five talents came and brought five other talents, saying, "Lord, you delivered to me five talents; look, I have gained five more talents besides them." His lord said to him, "Well done, good and faithful servant; you were faithful over a few things, I will make you ruler over many things. Enter into the joy of your lord." He also who had received two talents came and said, "Lord, you delivered to me two talents; look, I have gained two more talents besides them." His lord said to him, "Well done, good and faithful servant; you have been faith-

ful over a few things, I will make you ruler over many things. Enter into the joy of your lord" (Matthew 25:20-23).

Lord, Help me see my job as my ministry in life. May I do all my work to please You. Help me serve You by doing my job the very best I can do. Amen.

LEARNING TO WORK CHRISTIAN

When I (Dave) graduated from college, I won awards for preaching and for leadership. As I started seminary, I easily secured a part-time position at a church. But when my wife needed to quit her job so she could do her student teaching, I needed a second part-time job to provide for our family. I assumed employers would be delighted to hire me. Yet, at that time, the country was experiencing a recession, and jobs were especially scarce where we lived. After weeks of pounding the pavement, looking for part-time work, I finally found the only job available. I secured a part-time job on the cleaning staff of a very large church and Christian school.

I have to confess, I had been hoping to have my own office, not clean other people's offices. I thought my office suite may have its own bathroom, yet here I was cleaning bathrooms. I had hoped to be asked to preach from that church's pulpit, but now I was assigned to vacuum around it.

It was tough. I went to seminary all day and worked from 4:00 P.M. to 10:00 P.M., Monday through Friday. Saturday, I got up early and drove an hour to church where I was the youth, children, bus, and assistant pastor. Cathy and I worked at the church all day Saturday and Sunday. Then we got up and did it all over again on Monday.

At first I was embarrassed with being a lowly custodian and struggled with my attitude. Our boss would often give us our assignments then he would take off, never to be seen or heard from the rest of the night. I soon found myself grumbling about my boss, doing just enough to get by, and hating my job.

But after a few weeks of frustration, the Lord spoke to me as I was reading Colossians 3:22-24. I realized that I needed to see work in general, and that job in particular, as a gift from God. It paid the bills, allowed me to take my seminary classes, and gave me weekends free to serve in my church. I realized I needed to have a much better attitude about my boss. I needed to work much harder. Most of all, I needed to see this job as a wonderful opportunity to worship the Lord.

I determined that I would give the Lord the very best I could do.

There were 22 custodians on the staff (I told you it was a large church and school) and we were graded at the end of every week on how clean our areas were as they were inspected. At the beginning of the new week, the 22 custodians were ranked 1 through 20 based on the scores of our inspections.

After deciding that I needed to view this job as a ministry, I finished first or second every week. I also began to enjoy and even look forward to my job. I no longer was ashamed of my position as a custodian.

I had to learn that work is not so much a matter of having the right *position*, but that it is a matter of having the right *perspective* and being the right type of *person*. God is ultimately more interested in our character than our career.

Interestingly, after nine very tough months in that job, the Lord provided me with a much, much better job with its own office, great benefits, and wonderful ministry opportunities. As I look back, I wonder if I would have ever gotten the great job if I had not tried to be a responsible Christian worker on my not-so-great custodial job.

How to Pray About Your Job

Lord, thank You for the ability to work. May I be an authentic Christian worker. Please help me have a great attitude about my job and my boss. Help me recognize that You are my ultimate boss. Enable me to do my very best at all times. Help me do all work as a ministry to others and as an offering to You. Amen.

Good quote:

Once you realize how many different ways there are to influence your coworkers for Christ (without preaching a word), you'll be challenged to develop a lifestyle so striking and true, that the people you work with will be eager to let you talk about what makes you different.[7]

Questions for Thought

1. When a person is working in a terrible situation, what changes can be made to improve working conditions?

2. When a person "hates" his or her job, what can the person do about it?

3. If a person doesn't feel the job is a ministry, what should be done?

4. When a person isn't doing his or her best at a job, and is happy doing "second best," what can be done to change the worker's attitude?

5. What should a person do when stuck in a "dead-end" job?

6. Why is it some Christians are not the best workers, but some unsaved people are better workers and are more productive for the company?

ENDNOTES

1. Rick Warren, *The Purpose Driven Life* (Grand Rapids, MI: Zondervan, 2002), 67.

2. Randy Alcorn, *Safely Home* (Carol Stream, IL: Tyndale House, 2003), 270-272.

3. Ibid., 276-277.

4. ὑπακούω: hup (under) + akouo (listen), James Strong, *The New Strong's Exhaustive Concordance of the Bible*, Nashville, Thomas Nelson, 1990, entry G191.

5. ἐργάζεσθε, Strong's, G2038.

6. ψυχῆς, Strong's G1537.

7. Doug Sherman and William Hendricks, *Your Work Matters to God* (Colorado Springs, CO: NavPress, 1990), 254.

Chapter 6

Not Where but How—Becoming the Right Worker Before You Find the Right Job

Dave Earley

The reward for work well done is the opportunity to do more. —Jonas Salk

Lazy people are soon poor, hard workers get rich (Proverbs 10:4 TLB).

IT may surprise you to learn that God is not as concerned about *where* you work as He is about *how* you work. Your location is not as important as your disposition. Your career is not as significant as your character. Before we discuss how to pray about finding the right job, it is more important for us to learn to pray about how to become the right worker. Maybe God will not give you the right job until you make it a priority to become the right type of Christian worker.

WHICH TYPE OF WORKER AM I?

I love the Old Testament Book of Proverbs. It is a concise, "common sense" look at daily life. In it are verbal caricatures of a variety of common people. If you have worked around many different types of people in your life, you can read the Book of Proverbs and find them succinctly described. When it comes to the subject of "work," all of these characters fall into one of two groups—they are either good workers or bad ones. God is pleased with and blesses the noble workers and curses the rest.

As we study them, take inventory of your life and work habits. Are you the type of worker God delights in? Or are there some changes you need to be praying about?

The Lazy Worker

I love the way Proverbs pulls no punches in describing the lazy person. The Bible often describes the lazy person as a "sluggard" or a "sloth." Today we use the word *sloth* to also describe a slow-moving, sleepy, shaggy mammal of South and Central America that spends its life hanging upside down from a tree eating leaves. Sloths are neither cute nor interesting. No one writes fun children's stories about sloths. The term *slug* is worse. It is used to describe a small, elongated, slimy, slow-moving, shell-less, snail-like gastropod mollusk that crawls in the dirt. Yuck! No one wants to be a slug. If you want to insult someone, call him a slug.

Proverbs has much to say about slothful, lazy sluggards—and none of it is good. It is bad to be a lazy worker. Hopefully none of these characteristics are true of you:

1. They start slowly and end up in poverty.

How long will you slumber, O sluggard? When will you rise from your sleep? A little sleep, a little slumber, a little folding of the hands to sleep—So shall your poverty come on you like a prowler, and your need like an armed man (Proverbs 6:9-11).

2. Their wants will not be satisfied.

The soul of a lazy man desires, and has nothing... (Proverbs 13:4).

3. Their procrastination leads to their poverty.

I went by the field of the lazy man and by the vineyard of the man devoid of understanding; and there it was, all overgrown with thorns; its surface was covered with nettles; its stone wall was broken down. When I saw it, I considered it well; I looked on it and received instruction: A little sleep, a little slumber, a little folding of the hands to rest; so shall your poverty come like a prowler, and your need like an armed man (Proverbs 24:30-34).

4. They fail to finish tasks and miss out as a result.

The lazy man does not roast what he took in hunting... (Proverbs 12:27).

A lazy man buries his hand in the bowl, and will not so much as bring it to his mouth again (Proverbs 19:24).

5. They make excuses to avoid unpleasant tasks and end up regretting it.

The lazy man will not plow because of winter; he will beg during harvest and have nothing (Proverbs 20:4).

The lazy man says, "There is a lion outside! I shall be slain in the streets!" (Proverbs 22:13)

6.   They make things more difficult than they really are.

The way of the lazy man is like a hedge of thorns, but the way of the upright is a highway (Proverbs 15:19).

7.   Their laziness becomes an irritant to their employer and co-workers.

As vinegar to the teeth and smoke to the eyes, so is the lazy man to those who send him (Proverbs 10:26).

THE GREEDY

Work and wealth are gifts from God. But work and wealth by themselves always make very poor gods. Setting your heart on being rich will never lead to lasting fulfillment. Making work and wealth your gods ultimately lead to trouble for you and also the ones you love. Consider these truths:

1.   The greedy will be disillusioned when their wealth dries up.

Do not overwork to be rich; because of your own understanding, cease! Will you set your eyes on that which is not? For riches certainly make themselves wings; they fly away like an eagle toward heaven (Proverbs 23:4-5).

2.   The greedy will ultimately bring down their family.

He who is greedy for gain troubles his own house, but he who hates bribes will live (Proverbs 15:27).

3.   The greedy end up in pain of poverty or punishment.

He who trusts in his riches will fall... (Proverbs 11:28).

The faithful man will abound with blessings, but he who hastens to be rich will not go unpunished (Proverbs 28:20).

THE DECEITFUL WORKER

Some workers lie, cheat, swindle, and steal. At first they may seem to be gaining from it, but in the long run, it ultimately leads to their disillusionment, devastation, and downfall.

The wicked man does deceptive work, but he who sows righteousness will have a sure reward (Proverbs 11:18).

Stolen water is sweet, and bread eaten in secret is pleasant. But he does not know that the dead are there, that her guests are in the depths of hell (Proverbs 9:17-18).

Bread gained by deceit is sweet to a man, but afterward his mouth will be filled with gravel (Proverbs 20:17).

Wealth gained by dishonesty will be diminished... (Proverbs 13:11).

Getting treasures by a lying tongue is the fleeting fantasy of those who seek death (Proverbs 21:6).

The Diligent and Disciplined Worker

The soul of a lazy man desires, and has nothing; but the soul of the diligent shall be made rich (Proverbs 13:4).

Standing in stark contrast to the lazy worker is the diligent, disciplined worker. The word used for "diligent" is a word that was also used for a sharp, pointed threshing instrument used to cut corn. It also was used to describe cutting a clean trench for water to flow through. It could also be translated sharp, eager, and energetic. These Christian workers are fulfilled, succeed, and are blessed by God.

1. They succeed financially.

He who has a slack hand becomes poor, but the hand of the diligent makes rich (Proverbs 10:4).

2. They have their self-respect.

...but diligence is man's precious possession (Proverbs 12:27).

3. They will experience fulfillment in their work.

A desire accomplished is sweet to the soul… (Proverbs 13:19).

He who tills his land will be satisfied with bread… (Proverb 12:11).

4. They will be promoted.

The hand of the diligent will rule, but the lazy man will be put to forced labor (Proverbs 12:24).

The Thoughtful, Responsible Worker

We live in a crude, rude, throw-it-away society. Many in the workplace waste resources and use people. God blesses workers who are both thoughtful and responsible.

1. They care for the resources and people placed at their disposal.

A righteous man regards the life of his animal, but the tender mercies of the wicked are cruel (Proverbs 12:10).

2. They treat their subordinates respectfully.

Like a roaring lion and a charging bear is a wicked ruler over poor people. A ruler who lacks understanding is a great oppressor, but he who hates covetousness will prolong his days (Proverbs 28:15-16).

3. They take good care of their equipment and other resources.

Whoever keeps the fig tree will eat its fruit… (Proverbs 27:18).

4. They are sensitive to the needs of their boss.

…So he who waits on his master will be honored (Proverbs 27:18).

THE QUICK AND SKILLFUL WORKER

Do you see a man who excels in his work? He will stand before kings; he will not stand before unknown men (Proverbs 22:29).

The word rendered "excel" can also mean quick, prompt, skilled, ready. It describes speed, efficiency, and competence. Christian workers are to do the job, do it quickly, and do it well. As a result, they are rewarded.

THE FAITHFUL, LOYAL, DEPENDABLE WORKER

In a "me first," "every man for himself" world, faithful, loyal workers are rare jewels. Dependable employees are the type of Christian workers God enjoys blessing.

1. They quietly get the job done.

Most men will proclaim each his own goodness, but who can find a faithful man? (Proverbs 20:6)

2.   They can keep confidence.

A talebearer reveals secrets, but he who is of a faithful spirit conceals a matter (Proverbs 11:13).

3.   They make situations better, instead of making them worse.

A wicked messenger falls into trouble, but a faithful ambassador brings health (Proverbs 13:17).

4.   They are honest.

A faithful witness does not lie, but a false witness will utter lies (Proverbs 14:5).

5.   They are positive refreshment to their bosses.

Like the cold of snow in time of harvest is a faithful messenger to those who send him, for he refreshes the soul of his masters (Proverbs 25:13).

6.   They will end up being blessed.

A faithful man will abound with blessings, but he who hastens to be rich will not go unpunished (Proverbs 28:20).

What Does Your Boss Think of You?

Long ago, in the days before cell phones, the story was told of a young man who pulled into a gas station to use the pay phone.

Another man waiting behind him saw him put his coin in the phone and dial a number. Then the young man said, "Yes, I was calling about the position in your business that you advertised for last week. I was wondering if you were still looking for a diligent, dependable, honest, and skilled fellow to work for your company."

The man waiting in line could hear the reply through the receiver. "No, I'm sorry, but we already have one of those."

The young man broke into a wide grin and said, "Thanks," and hung up.

The man waiting in line asked the young man why he was so happy to hear that the position was not available.

"Because I am the one in that position," the young man replied. "I was just calling to see what my boss thought of me."

I wonder, what does your earthly boss think of you? Would he or she say that you are lazy, deceitful, or greedy? Or would your boss tell us that you are diligent, responsible, skilled, efficient, and faithful?

Even more importantly, how does your ultimate Boss, the Lord, view your work? Are you the type of Christian worker who blesses Him and someone He is glad to bless?

How to Pray for Your Job

Lord, help me be the right type of Christian worker. May my work habits positively reflect on my relationship with You. Help me work hard. Enable me to grow in speed, efficiency, and excellence. Help me be responsible with the resources You give me to do my job and to be thoughtful of the people I serve and who work under me. May You be honored as others find me dependable, loyal, and faithful. Lord, help me become the right type of Christian worker so You can ultimately guide me to the right job. Amen.

Questions for Thought

1. How often is there conflict between the boss's opinion of a person's job and the worker's opinion? What causes the conflict? If that's your situation, what can you do about it?

2. What makes some workers "lazy?" How can you make sure you are not lazy?

3. What makes some workers "greedy?" What should you do when you become aware of "greed" in your motivations?

4. What makes some workers more diligent than others? What can you do to make sure you work as diligently as possible?

5. What makes some workers deceitful in their work habits, and what makes them lie on the job? How can you make sure you are a truthful person?

6. The Bible commends the faithful, dependable, loyal workers. What can you do to fit that qualification?

Chapter 7

The Fourfold Prayer You Should Pray for Your Job Every Day

Dave Earley

If people had to walk to work, they would fuss and complain every step of the way. But when they go to play 18 holes of golf, they enjoy every mile they walk.
—David Benoit

Pray as though everything depended on God. Work as though everything depended on you. —Saint Augustine

Bless me indeed…enlarge my territory…keep me from evil that I may not cause pain! (1 Chronicles 4:10)

"SURELY I was born for more than this."

Sound familiar? Maybe you go to work each day with a gnawing hunger and restless burden of wanting to do more and be more for God. If so, you are not alone. You were created with the craving to work in order to create a better world.

God is the giver and fulfiller of dreams. I believe that at conception He begins writing dreams on each of our hearts. These deep dreams perfectly wed His purposes on the planet with the passion of our souls. In your heart today are the seeds of greater works that

God wants to work through you tomorrow. God planted them there. They are a secret of your fulfillment.

One man took a risk and acted on his God-given ambitions. His name was Jabez. His story has been widely publicized recently in Christian circles. Interestingly, the Bible record of Jabez is condensed into four short sentences found in two simple verses.

Now Jabez was more honorable than his brothers, and his mother called his name Jabez, saying, "Because I bore him in pain." And Jabez called on the God of Israel saying, "Oh, that You would bless me indeed, and enlarge my territory, that Your hand would be with me, and that You would keep me from evil, that I may not cause pain!" So God granted him what he requested (1 Chronicles 4:9-10).

God summarized the entire life of Jabez into four facts:

1. Jabez was more honorable than his brothers.

2. He received his name, Jabez, because his mother gave birth to him in pain.

3. He asked God to give him his fourfold dream of blessing, enlargement, presence, and protection.

4. God answered, "Yes!" Jabez's prayer is one of the most effective prayers in the Bible. We are not told *how* God answered, but we are clearly told *that* God granted his request.

Likewise, Jabez's request was fourfold:

1. Bless me.

2.   Enlarge my territory.

3.   Let Your hand be with me.

4.   Keep me from harm so that I will be free from pain.

When I read this request by Jabez, I find myself yearning for the same thing. But is it selfish or arrogant to ask God for that? The first time I read this verse, I assumed that God would say, "You have got to be kidding!"

But He didn't. God took the sincere cry of Jabez's heart seriously. So I figure if God would do such a thing for Jabez, He might do it for me. And He has, as I have prayed this fourfold request for my work daily.

THE FOURFOLD PRAYER YOU SHOULD PRAY FOR YOUR JOB EVERY DAY

Bless Me

*And Jabez called on the God of Israel saying, "Oh, that You would **bless me** indeed...." So God granted him what he requested* (1 Chronicles 4:10).

According to Bruce Wilkinson, writing in *The Prayer of Jabez*, "The very nature of God is to have goodness in so much abundance that it overflows into our unworthy lives. If you think about God differently than that, I am asking you to change the way you think. Why not make it a lifelong commitment to ask God every day to bless you—while He's at it, bless you *a lot*."[1]

When Jabez prayed, "Bless me," we do know that the Lord did indeed answer his request. But we do not know *how* the Lord answered. But Jabez was not the first to offer this request. Years earlier a man named Jacob offered the same petition to the same Lord.

You probably know the story. Jacob was "in a heap of trouble," in the form of his wild, strong, angry, murderous brother Esau. Years before, Jacob had taken the birthright blessing meant for his older brother, Esau, and Esau had not forgotten.

Esau was bearing down on Jacob with an army of 400 men. At that point Jacob did what desperate men should do. He prayed (see Gen. 32:9-12), but he didn't sound very sincere, apparently even to himself. Thus, he continued to try and wiggle out of sure disaster (see Gen. 32:13-24), and ended up finding himself alone and even more desperate (see Gen. 32:24).

Then a man appeared in the dark to Jacob, and a wrestling match began. Arms were twisted, legs were seized, and necks were wrenched. All through the night, hand-to-hand combat was waged. When it became clear Jacob could not win, he grabbed hold of the stranger and hung on for dear life. Then he uttered a small prayer: *"I will not let You go unless You bless me!"* (Gen. 32:26).

Jacob had taken hold of God—his opponent in the dark—and refused to let go until God blessed him. Asking for all of the blessing he could get was typical of Jacob. He had asked his father to give him the biggest blessing his father could give and now he was asking the same of God.

When I first read this story I was surprised at the boldness, the brashness, and yes, the greediness of Jacob. Come on! I was expecting God to rise up and blast him for making such a request. Instead, God gave Jacob what he asked for. God blessed him with a manifold blessing:

1. Transformation: Jacob got a new name to signify his new heart—Israel. He would no longer be Jacob—"grasper, deceiver, schemer," but would now be Israel—"prevailer, prince" (see Gen. 32:27-28).

2. Revelation: Jacob got a new, personal experience with and understanding of God. It was so real that he named the place Peniel—"the face of God" (see Gen. 32:29-32).

3. Direction: God gave Jacob a plan based on humility and generosity, instead of strength and greed. This plan won his brother's heart (see Gen. 32:3).

4. Protection: Esau's heart was so changed that when he saw Jacob, instead of killing him, he embraced him and kissed him. Together they wept. Years of deep bitterness and guilt were erased in a few moments. God had blessed Jacob with protection in the face of sure death (see Gen. 33:4).

5. Impact: This little prayer caused lives to be changed! All those with Jacob—his wives, children, servants, and livestock—were spared, including Judah, from whom the Messiah would descend. So, in a sense, Jacob's prayer blessed all of us. Beyond that, Esau's life was wonderfully altered. He let go of a lifetime of bitterness toward his overly aggressive brother. Instead

of killing Jacob, he embraced him. Yet, the biggest change was seen in the life of Jacob. Jacob not only had a new name, but he had a new heart, one of generosity (see Gen. 33:8-11). His final words to Esau were these, *"Please, take my blessing that is brought to you, because God has dealt graciously with me, and because I have enough…"* (Gen. 33:11).

Can you imagine Jacob begging Esau to "please take my blessing?" Jacob, the one who previously had stolen the blessing, was now eager to give a blessing. He was a new man. He humbly acknowledged that God had blessed him. Therefore, he desired to bless others.

"Bless me that I might bless others."

The point of blessing must not be selfish. God is all about others. Everything He does in us and for us is designed to eventually flow through us to others. God gives the most to those with the most open hands. God blesses us so that we will bless others.

My dad was a Christian businessman who did business with diligence, integrity, and reverence for Christ. As a small business owner, he suffered through some very lean years. Later in his life, he began to pray, "Lord, bless me that I might bless others." God answered his request and Dad did his part.

As a result, his business grew and flourished. He had a very healthy income and was giving a large part of it away. He and my mother tithed to two churches, and regularly and generously supported 20 other Christian ministries. They also gave hundreds of dollars away monthly to students and families in need.

Through the years, as the Lord has blessed me with positions of influence, I have been blessed to bless others. I use my position to bless others in many ways including: jobs; references; arranging for hard-to-make introductions; networking; cutting through red tape by making strategic phone calls; linking partnerships; sharing experience and advice; and giving necessary direction and encouragement.

Enlarge My Territory

And Jabez called on the God of Israel saying, "Oh, that You would bless me indeed, and **enlarge my territory….***" So God granted him what he requested* (1 Chronicles 4:10).

When Jabez prayed, *"enlarge my territory"* we know that the Lord did indeed answer his request. But again we do not know *how* the Lord answered. Asking God to enlarge our territory is not something we should feel guilty about. With the right motives, it can leave a powerful testimony with the world. According to Henry Blackaby:

God is interested in the world coming to know him. The only way people will know him is when they see him at work. Whenever God involves you in his activity, the assignment will have God-like dimensions to it. Some people say, 'God will never ask me to do something I can't do.' I have come to the place in my life that, if the assignment I sense God is giving me is something I can handle, I know it probably is not from God. The kind of assignments God gives…are always beyond what people can do because he wants to demonstrate His nature, His strength, His provision, and His kindness to His people and to a watching world. That is the only way the world will come to know Him.... When God's people and the world see something happen that only God can do, they come to know Him."[2]

When we ask God to enlarge our territory, we are asking God to increase our sphere of influence for His Kingdom. Bruce Wilkinson helps us understand how this prayer works:

If Jabez had worked on Wall Street, he might have prayed, "Lord increase the value of my investments/ portfolios." When I talk to presidents of companies, I often talk to them in terms of this particular mind-set. When Christian executives ask me, "Is it right for me to ask for more business?" my response is, "Absolutely!" If you're doing business God's way, it's not only right to ask for more, but He is waiting for you to ask. Your business is God's territory that God has entrusted to you. He wants you to accept it as a significant opportunity to touch individual lives, the business community, and the world for His glory. Asking Him to enlarge that opportunity brings Him only delight."[3]

When we ask for more territory, we are tapping into the heart of Jesus, whose heart was so large it encompassed the whole world. Among His final words to His followers was to *make disciples of **all** the nations*" (Matt. 28:19); to *preach the good news to **all** creation*" (Mark 16:15); that *repentance and forgiveness of sins be preached in His name to **all** nations*" (Luke 24:47 TLB); and for His followers to be *witnesses to Me in Jerusalem, and in **all** Judea and Samaria, and to the ends of the earth*" (Acts 1:8). Notice the word *all* in each reference.

Part of the world was not enough. *Some* of the people won't do. He wanted His kingdom, His territory, to extend to *all* the people in the world.

"Give Me This Mountain"

When we ask God to expand our territory, we are standing on the shoulders of spiritual giants. At the age of 85, Joshua's visionary buddy Caleb was not ready to retire, nor was he content with the status quo. He asked for greater territory.

*And now, behold, the Lord has kept me alive, as He said, these forty-five years, ever since the Lord spoke this word to Moses while Israel wandered in the wilderness; and now, here I am this day, eighty-five years old. As yet I am as strong this day as on the day that Moses sent me; just as my strength was then, so now is my strength for war, both for going out and for coming in. Now therefore, **give me this mountain** of which the Lord spoke in that day…* (Joshua 14:10-12).

Enlarge my territory is a prayer God loves to answer. Henrietta Mears was a big dreamer. At the age of 38, she took the position of Director of Christian Education at the First Presbyterian Church in Hollywood, California. "God doesn't call us to sit on the sidelines and watch. He calls us to be on the field, playing the games," said Ms. Mears. Knowing Christ intimately and telling others about Him was her first and foremost objective.

Three years after her arrival at the church, Sunday school attendance grew from 400 to 4,000. Over 400 young people entered full-time Christian service during her tenure. One of them was Bill Bright, founder of Campus Crusade for Christ.

God kept expanding her territory. Frustrated with the material being taught in the Sunday school when she arrived, she began to write lessons that would honor Christ and be faithful to the Bible. It wasn't long before her efforts gained results and requests for copies of her material came in from all across the country. Her office staff worked many long hours mimeographing and mailing the lessons. When the demand became too great, Mears and a group of businesspeople established Gospel Light Publications, one of the largest evangelical publishers in the Christian education field.

For years, Mears searched for a retreat area where she could take her high school and college-aged students. She asked God to provide for her dream. Soon, a privately owned resort in the San Bernardino Mountains was available, but the price was too high. For a moment, the dream appeared impossible. Mears called a group of people together for prayer. She insisted that they should "dream big whenever God was involved," and trust Him for His blessing at the right time. After a miraculous intervention, Forest Home, valued at $350,000, was purchased in 1938 for the unheard of price of $30,000.

God expanded her territory into unique realms. Initially, Mears had been drawn to California for the opportunity to witness to those in the entertainment industry. God provided an open door into this area through the Hollywood Christian Group, which began meeting in her home. Many entertainment professionals came to know Christ as a result of her ministry. Dozens of Christian leaders acknowledge her as well, including Billy Graham who said of her, "I doubt if any other woman outside my wife and mother has had such a marked influence [on my life]."[4]

Be With Me

*And Jabez called on the God of Israel saying, "Oh, that You would bless me indeed, and enlarge my territory, that Your hand would **be with me**...." So God granted him what he requested* (1 Chronicles 4:10).

When Jabez prayed *"be with me,"* we know that the Lord did indeed answer his request. But we do not know *how* the Lord answered. He understood what many effective Christian workers have understood through the years—God's presence makes all the difference.

Take Joseph, for example. His jealous brothers had thrown him into a pit, then sold him into slavery. He ended up in a foreign land working for Pharaoh's captain of the guard, Potiphar. Note how the Lord's presence brought Joseph success in his work.

The Lord was with Joseph, and he was a successful man; and he was in the house of his master the Egyptian. And his master saw that the Lord was with him and that the Lord made all he did to prosper in his hand. So Joseph found favor in his sight, and served him. Then he made him overseer of his house, and all that he had he put under his authority. So it was, from the time that he had made him overseer of his house and all that he had, that the Lord blessed the Egyptian's house for Joseph's sake;

and the blessing of the Lord was on all that he had in the house and in the field (Genesis 39:2-5).

You probably are familiar with the story. Potiphar's lustful wife tried unsuccessfully to seduce Joseph into sleeping with her. When he refused, she made up a lie and got Joseph thrown in prison on an attempted rape charge. But again God's presence brought Joseph prosperity in his work.

*But **the Lord was with** Joseph and showed him mercy, and He gave him favor in the sight of the keeper of the prison. And the keeper of the prison committed to Joseph's hand all the prisoners who were in the prison; whatever they did there, it was his doing. The keeper of the prison did not look into anything that was under Joseph's authority, because **the Lord was with him;** and whatever he did, the Lord made it prosper* (Genesis 39:21-23).

Consider Moses. He faced one of the most difficult leadership challenges in history. He had to lead a million whining slaves out of Egypt, through the desert wilderness, and into the Promised Land. Every time he turned around, his people were either rebelling or griping.

One of the lowest points came when Moses descended from Mount Sinai carrying the Ten Commandments, only to come upon a riotous party at which the people were worshiping idols. God would have annihilated the Hebrew people had Moses not interceded (see Exod. 32:9-14). How was Moses supposed to guide the people safely through the hazards of the desert into the Promised Land without them destroying him or themselves?

Moses wisely established a strong prayer life. He met with the Lord daily in what he called the *"tent of meeting"* (Exod. 33:7-11). Moses desperately needed the presence of God. There was no other way. Yet he not only recognized his need, he acted on it. Moses was ultimately successful because he asked God for help, praying one of the most effective prayers in the Bible.

> *You have said, "I know you by name and you have found favor with Me. If You are pleased with me, teach me Your ways so I may know You and continue to find favor with You. Remember that this nation is Your people." The Lord replied, "My Presence will go with you, and I will give you rest." Then Moses said to him, "If Your Presence does not **go with us**, do not send us up from here"* (Exodus 33:12-15 NIV).

"If Your Presence does not go with us, do not send us up from here." In other words, "Your presence is the key to our peace, protection, and prosperity. Go with us. Your presence is the source of our survival and success. Without You there will soon be none of us." Moses prayed, *"Go with us."* He was saying, "Lord, Your presence is the mark of Your pleasure. Your attendance sets us apart. You are distinctly divine. Without You we are nothing but a tragic troop tramping aimlessly into oblivion."

So Moses asked God to go with them. And God said, "Yes."

And the Lord said to Moses, "I will do the very thing you have asked, because I am pleased with you and I know you by name" (Exodus 33:17 NIV).

From that moment, God's presence marked Moses' life. In fact, God was so manifestly with him that Moses' face actually glowed. Eventually the impossible task of establishing the rabble of Hebrew slaves into a nation and guiding them into the Promised Land became a reality. God's presence made the difference.

What You Need Most Is GOD!

A few years ago as I was reading the Bible, I discovered that embedded in the defining moments of the lives of key people in the Bible is the little phrase, "God was with him." God's presence was the determining factor.

The things we want and need most in life come from God. They are only realized when His presence is manifest with us. Read down through the following "grocery list" of the staggering blessings and benefits attending God's people when He accompanies them.

- Individual protection and provision—Gen. 28:15,20.

- Deliverance and transformation—Acts 7:9.

- Prosperity in the face of grave adversity—Gen. 39:2.

- Favor with ungodly authorities—Gen. 39:21.

- Success—Gen. 39:23; 1 Sam. 18:12,14; 1 Chron. 17:2; 2 Kings 18:7.

- National protection—Num. 14:8.

- Blessings—Num. 23:21.

- Destruction of fear—Deut. 31:6,8; Josh. 1:9; Ps. 118:6.

- Godly influence—Josh. 6:27.

- Courage—Judg. 6:12.

- Victory—Judg. 1:19,22; Isa. 8:10.

- Guarantee of God's promises—1 Sam. 3:19.

- Transformation and power—1 Sam. 10:6-7.

- Qualification for leadership—1 Sam. 16:18.

- Greatness—2 Sam. 7:9; 2 Chron. 1:1; 1 Kings 1:37.

- Encouragement—1 Chron. 28:20.

- Magnetic ability to draw a large following—2 Chron. 15:9.

- Confidence—Ps. 118:7; 2 Chron. 13:12; Jer. 20:11; Zech. 10:5.

- Evident favor of God—Luke 1:28.

- Miraculous power—Acts 10:38.

I say, sign me up! No wonder Jabez prayed, "Be with me."

Protect Me, Keep Me From Evil

And Jabez called on the God of Israel saying, "Oh, that You would bless me indeed, and enlarge my territory, that Your hand would be with me, and that You would **keep me from** *evil, that I may not cause pain!"* So God granted him what he requested (1 Chronicles 4:10).

Jabez's fourth request was to be kept from evil. One thing he understood was pain. The name Jabez means "pain." He was born out of his mother's extreme pain. He had seen plenty of pain in his life. So he asked God to protect him from evil.

Translators are not definite on exactly what sort of protection Jabez was seeking. However, I think that the protection he wanted was from committing evil. He realized that if he gave in to temptation, it would hurt others. He had experienced enough pain that he did not want to cause anyone else to experience any more.

Remember that Jesus taught His followers to pray, *"And do not lead us into temptation, but deliver us from the evil one"* (Matt. 6:13). I think that Jabez was saying to the Lord, "Protect me from temptation, and the pain that giving in to it would cause others."

Every job can be a landmine of temptation. We may be tempted to take company property. We may be tempted to steal company time by doing personal business while we are being paid to work. We may be tempted to mistreat a co-worker or a subordinate. There is temptation to enter into the latest office gossip or slander or griping session. Maybe the temptation is to develop an improper romantic attachment with a co-worker. Or the temptation is to walk on someone else's back as you try to climb the corporate ladder. We must resist temptation, not only for our sakes, but also for the sakes of others.

GOD PROMISES A WAY OF ESCAPE

No temptation has overtaken you except such as is common to man; but God is faithful, who will not allow you to be tempted beyond what you are able, but with the temptation will also make the way of escape, that you may be able to bear it (1 Corinthians 10:13).

Note that the promise is not that we won't be tempted. We will. Count on it. Until we get to Heaven we will be tempted. It is a fact of life. Rather, the promise is that we won't face any temptation that is more than we can handle with God's help.

Temptation is a deadly predator that is out to get you. It is cunning and shrewd. One moment its advance is subtle and apparently innocent. The next, it rises up and assaults with overwhelming force. This soul seducer can present itself as harmless as a lamb, but it has the bite of a viper. It is both too beautiful to resist and too powerful to deny.

You cannot let up because your assailant won't. This relentless raider is always on the attack, never taking a break, never going on a vacation, and never taking a day off. Be aware. Like a cagey boxer, this adversary will size you up quickly, diagnose your weaknesses, wait for the opening or fake you into letting down your guard, and then *BAM!* It will drop you with an unexpected blow. Stay alert.

Temptation is a fierce foe. And it's after you. That's the bad news. The good news is that no matter how severe the temptation, you don't have to give in.

You Are Not Alone

"No temptation has overtaken you except such as is common to man." Often when we are tempted, we think that we are the only one facing temptation. But that is simply not true. Humans have been facing temptation since the Garden of Eden. We all face it. Even Jesus faced temptation. It is part and parcel of the human condition on planet Earth.

Temptation is no respecter of persons. It comes after children and adults, men and women, the lost and the saved, the spiritually young and the spiritually mature. Pastors and missionaries face temptations just as often as anyone else. When you battle with temptation, you are not alone.

When tempted, we also tend to assume that we are the only one facing this type, or level, of temptation. Again, not true. Every sin imaginable has been around as long as there have been people to commit it. While you are undoubtedly a unique and special person, you are not facing a unique or special temptation.

It's Not Irresistible

"But God is faithful, who will not allow you to be tempted beyond what you are able." This is the promise and the good news. No temptation is irresistible. Let me repeat that. No temptation is irresistible. God will not allow any unbearable seduction to enter our lives.

Note carefully that the basis for the ability to resist temptation is not *our* strength, wisdom, or will power. Rather, it is *God's* faithfulness.

He is the power needed to say "No" to sin. He gives us the ability to refuse temptation.

I might need to clarify that temptation, in and of itself, is not sin. Temptation is the *appeal to* sin. It is possible to be tempted and not sin. The thought of sin is not sin until it is entertained and acted on. Alone in the wilderness, the sinless One, Jesus Himself, the holy Son of God, was tempted three times; yet all three times He refused (see Matt. 4:1-11). And He gives us the power to resist temptation. He who resisted temptation can give us victory over temptation.

No Excuse

"But with the temptation will also make the way of escape, that you may be able to bear it." For the child of God, there is never an excuse for sin. There is always a way to avoid it. God will provide a way to avoid it or the power to resist it. That is His promise. But while it is God's responsibility to give us a way out, it is our responsibility to take it. We must take the escape route.

How to Pray About Your Job

Lord, thank You for my job. Today, I ask You to bless me. Pour out Your favor on my efforts and help me use those blessings to bless others. I ask You to enlarge my territory. Help me take more ground for You and Your Kingdom. Please be with me. If You don't go with me, I don't want to go. I need You. May Your presence be obviously manifested in and on my life. Keep me from evil. Protect me. Lead me not into temptation, but deliver me from evil and the evil one. Amen.

QUESTIONS FOR THOUGHT

1. Is the Jabez prayer something you should pray every day? Why would this be a good prayer?

2. Does the Jabez prayer deal with your attitude or your productivity? Which is more important?

3. God is concerned about the problems in Christian or church work, but is God concerned with problems at your job? Can you pray about them? Can you follow biblical principles to solve them?

4. How can God keep you from temptation and/or evil?

5. Will God bless you at work if you don't use His blessings to bless others? How can you do that?

ENDNOTES

1. Bruce Wilkinson, *The Prayer of Jabez* (Sisters, OR: Multnomah Publishers, 2000), 28-29.

2. Henry Blackaby and Claude King, *Experiencing God* (Nashville, TN: Broadman and Holman, 1995), 138.

3. Wilkinson, 31-32.

4. "Henrietta Mears: Dream Big," In Touch Ministries, www.intouch.org/myintouch/mighty/portraits/henrietta_mears_213642 (accessed November 28, 2004). Webpage no longer available.

Chapter 8

Examples of How to Get Your Job Done Better—From Bible Illustrations

Dave Earley

We work to become, not to acquire. —Elbert Hubbard

Let Your servant prosper this day, I pray, and grant me Your favor (Nehemiah 1:11 ELT).

THROUGH the years, one of the true joys in my prayer life has come from praying the actual prayers of the Bible, especially those that worked. I reason that if God answered the petitions of people like Jabez and Jacob, He might do the same for me—and He has!

Four of these prayers are especially appropriate as we pray about our jobs. They are petitions God enjoyed enough to have recorded as Scripture. They changed the lives of those who prayed them. They are requests that I make daily as I pray about my job.

NEHEMIAH'S PRAYERS REGARDING HIS JOB

Two of my daily job requests come from the life of a man named Nehemiah. As the cupbearer for King Artaxerxes, Nehemiah held a very responsible position, yet he longed to be 800 miles away, back with his people in the destroyed city of Jerusalem. They were facing possible annihilation, and Nehemiah needed to return to rebuild the city walls. More specifically, he needed three years off from his job and enough supplies to rebuild a wall around the entire city of Jerusalem! First, though, a huge change had to happen in the heart of the man in authority, that is, King Artaxerxes. Nehemiah's boss, an unbeliever, had a nasty reputation for cutting the heads off subordinates who upset him. For Nehemiah to march into the king's oval office and demand time off and building materials would be signing his own death warrant. So what could he do? He prayed.

GIVE ME FAVOR

O Lord, I pray, please let Your ear be attentive to the prayer of Your servant, and to the prayer of Your servants who desire to fear Your name; and let Your servant prosper this day, I pray, and **grant him mercy** [**favor**] *in the sight of this man* (Nehemiah 1:11).

Nehemiah's petition was that God would grant him favor by touching the king's heart in such a way as to give favor to Nehemiah and give him what he needed. Nehemiah was going to ask the king to send him off with his blessing to rebuild the walls *and* for the resources to pay for it!

The nature, size, and scope of Nehemiah's request were such that the odds of Artaxerxes saying "Yes" were slim. That's why Nehemiah went to God first. God would have to touch the king's heart *before* the king would ever agree to Nehemiah's petition. And He did. Listen to Nehemiah tell what happened.

> *Then the king said to me (the queen also sitting beside him), "How long will your journey be? And when will you return?" So it pleased the king to send me; and I set him a time. Furthermore I said to the king, "If it pleases the king, let letters be given to me for the governors of the region beyond the River, that they must permit me to pass through till I come to Judah, and a letter to Asaph the keeper of the king's forest, that he must give me timber to make beams for the gates of the citadel which pertains to the temple, for the city wall, and for the house that I will occupy." And the king granted them to me according to the good hand of my God upon me. Then I went to the governors in the region beyond the River, and gave them the king's letters. Now the king had sent captains of the army and horsemen with me* (Nehemiah 2:6-9).

The king gave Nehemiah all he asked for *plus* an army escort! Coincidence? No way. Nehemiah knew why the king showed him such incredible favor. He said it was because the gracious hand of his God was upon him.

Gaining the favor of Artaxerxes was a big obstacle to Nehemiah, but the power of Nehemiah's God dwarfed it. The king's heart was putty in God's hands. Nehemiah received exceedingly and abundantly more than he had asked or thought.

Often on our jobs we need favor with our superiors or with people in other departments to get things done. That's why we should ask God for it every day.

God *is* willing and able to change the hearts of those in authority. A friend who serves as an associate pastor recently told me how discouraged he had been by the refusal of his church's leadership to allow him to make necessary changes in the way the church did ministry. After the friend patiently prayed for favor, though, God touched their hearts and the changes are taking place. On top of that, he received a promotion and a raise!

STRENGTHEN MY HANDS

Often the task of doing excellent work as a Christian worker is overwhelming. We face opposition from without and weariness from within. We feel worn down, worn out, and weak. But we are not the first to feel this way.

Long ago, Nehemiah was working for brutally long days, week after week, trying to rebuild the walls of Jerusalem. He was attempting the impossible. His task was to lead a rag-tag remnant of God's people in the impossible task of rebuilding a structure that had lain in shambles for years.

All during the weeks of work, Nehemiah faced a strong enemy named Sanballat, who along with his friends, had attempted to discourage Nehemiah and his workers by laughing at their vision (see Neh. 2:19) and later criticizing and belittling their efforts (see Neh. 4:1-3). When that failed, they gathered a coalition force to try to frighten and intimidate the workers with the threat of a surprise attack (see Neh. 4:7-12). On top of that, there was division in the ranks of Nehemiah's workforce (see Neh. 5:1-13). Yet, through it all, Nehemiah's integrity, courage, and God-focused encouragement kept the work moving ahead until the walls were nearly completed.

Nearing the end, Nehemiah desperately needed some relief and rest. Instead, things got worse. Before he could catch his breath, his cunning nemesis, Sanballat, tried a new approach. Repeatedly, he requested meetings with Nehemiah. Yet Nehemiah wisely refused each request, sensing that Sanballat wanted, at the very least, to distract him from the task, and at the worst, hoped to kidnap or kill him.

After four refusals, Sanballat launched a new scheme. He cleverly misrepresented Nehemiah's motives, character, and methods in an open letter. In it, Sanballat even stated that Nehemiah was rebuilding the wall to make himself rich and powerful. These unsubstantiated and inaccurate rumors were designed to undercut Nehemiah's authority (see Neh. 6:5-7).

Yet, Nehemiah would not quit.

Note that God does not make it easy on His people. Just because we are trying to do as God wants does not mean that we will be immune to problems, frustrations, and attacks. Just the opposite is true.

Yet, Nehemiah fought on by fighting from his knees. He turned his problems into prayer. *"...Now therefore, O God, strengthen my hands"* (Neh. 6:9).

Nehemiah did not ask God to wipe out his enemies, as I might have done. He did not ask God to give this daunting responsibility to someone else, which I almost surely would have. He did not even ask for the walls to be miraculously built by legions of angels overnight, which I would at least have tried. Instead, he prayed, *"strengthen my hands."*

Sometimes God prefers to do the miracle *in* us.

Nehemiah prayed, *"strengthen my hands"* and God did.

So the wall was completed on the twenty-fifth of Elul, in fifty-two days (Nehemiah 6:15).

The wall was completed in a mere 52 days! No one would have believed it possible. Engineers still marvel at the accomplishment. Mission Impossible became Mission Accomplished! And make no mistake—this material structure was the result of spiritual activity. Prayer guided, fueled, forced, and completed the impossible. Nehemiah refused to quit, and God did not fail to bless. Yet, that's not all. When God gave Nehemiah strength to complete the project, his enemies became so discouraged that they were led to acknowledge that the rebuilding of the walls was the work of God!

And it happened, when all our enemies heard of it, and all the nations around us saw these things, that they were very disheartened in their own eyes; for they perceived that this work was done by our God (Nehemiah 6:16).

Nehemiah was not the first to ask God for strength, nor is he the last. The psalmist wrote:

God is our refuge and strength, a very present help in trouble (Psalm 46:1).

My flesh and my heart fail; but God is the strength of my heart and my portion forever (Psalm 73:26).

"Strengthen Me"

You remember the story of Samson, the world's strongest man. He forfeited his strength when he lost his connection to God, courtesy of his fateful haircut in Delilah's beauty salon (see Judg. 16:4-21). This led to the dual humiliation of his blinding and imprisonment.

You might not recall the rest of the story. The Philistines were having a party in honor of their god, Dagon, and they brought Samson out to entertain the guests. After he was finished, they chained him between the pillars of the great temple to Dagon. Then Samson did something he should have been doing all along (see Judg. 16:23-27). He prayed.

*Then Samson called to the Lord, saying, "O Lord God, remember me, I pray! **Strengthen me,** I pray, just this once, O God, that I may with one blow take vengeance on the Philistines for my two eyes!" (Judges 16:28)*

God did. In his death, Samson realized his greatest triumph.

If the Lord is strong enough to strengthen the hands of Nehemiah and merciful enough to strengthen the hands of Samson, then He can certainly give you the strength you need to serve Him on your job.

ABRAHAM'S SERVANT'S PRAYERS REGARDING HIS JOB

Give Me Success Today

Has your boss ever given you a seemly impossible task? What do you do when the expectations far surpass your ability to meet them?

The answer is pray for success. Let me explain.

When patriarch Abraham was the ripe old age of 140 years, his beloved wife, Sarah, passed away. Abraham seriously wanted his son, Isaac, to marry and give him a grandson. Isaac was already 40 years old and hopelessly single. So Abraham took action.

Abraham called his chief servant and sent him on an ancient version of Mission Impossible. He would have to travel 450 rigorous miles by camel to the area where Abraham grew up. There he was to select a suitable bride for Isaac. She would have to be from among Abraham's distant relatives (the custom was to marry a first cousin). After finding such a girl, he would then have to convince her to return with him to marry Isaac, a man she had never met. This would be no walk in the park.

The servant gathered a small caravan and made the lengthy trek to Abraham's homeland. His plan was to find the right girl at the central meeting place for desert communities—the well. As he approached the town, he offered a simple prayer:

> Then he said, "O Lord God of my master Abraham, please **give me success this day**, and show kindness to my master Abraham" (Genesis 24:12).

Notice the core of his prayer: "Give me success today." This request was simple, specific, and definite in reference to time. He asked God to direct him to the right girl and do it right away. After all, Isaac was not getting any younger. In order to know which girl would be the right one, the servant added to his request that she not merely offer to get him a drink *but also* volunteer to water his camels.

Behold, here I stand by the well of water, and the daughters of the men of the city are coming out to draw water. Now let it be that the young woman to whom I say, "Please let down your pitcher that I may drink," and she says, "Drink, and I will also give your camels a drink"—let her be the one You have appointed for Your servant Isaac. And by this I will know that You have shown kindness to my master (Genesis 24:13-14).

"Give me success today" was a little prayer. Yet it immediately reaped a stupendous, prodigious answer! Look at the glorious results:

*And it happened, **before he had finished speaking**, that behold, **Rebekah**, who was born to Bethuel, son of Milcah, the wife of Nahor, Abraham's brother, came out with her pitcher on her shoulder. Now the young woman was very beautiful to behold, a virgin; no man had known her. And she went down to the well, filled her pitcher, and came up. And the servant ran to meet her and said, "Please let me drink a little water from your pitcher." So she said, "Drink, my lord." Then she quickly let her pitcher down to her hand, and gave him a drink. And when she had finished giving him a drink, she said, "**I will draw water for*** *your camels also, until they have finished drinking"* (Genesis 24:15-19).

Bingo! God hit the target. He answered the servant's prayer and then some. *Before he had finished praying,* God sent the right girl— Rebekah, as it turned out, was a distant relative of Abraham, which meant she was qualified. Not insignificantly, she also happened to be a very beautiful and unattached virgin. To top it off, she not only gave the servant a drink, but she also offered to water his camels!

And that's not all. Later we read that Rebekah was willing to leave her family and her home immediately to make the return trip with the servant (see Gen. 24:58). The story even has a happy ending—when Isaac met her, he loved her (see Gen. 24:67).

Furthermore, God's "Yes" blessed everyone involved. Abraham had the good fortune of gaining a non-Canaanite daughter-in-law to be mother of his grandson. Rebekah became an essential part of God's promise to Abraham that he would become the father of many nations. For Rebekah, she received a husband who loved her and a place in the royal line of the Messiah. She moved from a pagan family to a God-fearing one. Isaac's life was changed because he received a very beautiful bride. Rebekah would be the woman he would love and who would bear his sons.

But the greatest windfall came to the servant. Prior to this event, the servant viewed God solely as Abraham's God. Instead of a personal relationship with the Lord, he had more of a secondhand relationship. But after he experienced the loving and powerful way God answered his prayer, he became a man who worshiped God for himself (see Gen. 24:26-27).

You Can Pray for Success on Your Job

Now the way I figure it, if God would do that for a servant whose name is not even recorded in the Bible, when he prayed, "*Give me success,*" how much will He do for you and me who are His own children!

I began praying this prayer when I accepted a new job as a professor several years ago. I had never been a professor before and was expected to start low on the totem pole. But every morning I prayed for success. God answered. Soon I was promoted to chairman over many senior faculty members.

On top of that, I was placed over the seminary's ministry department. It had been struggling, but over the next few years it exploded in impact and effectiveness. Beyond that, our fund-raising efforts for the seminary reaped huge rewards even in tough financial times.

Best of all, when I was hired at the seminary, I was asked to establish a Center of Church Planting from scratch. I was disappointed that after arriving on campus, I could find no one interested in church planting.

As we worked harder and smarter, and prayed for success, God blessed. All of the combined church and school entities had produced 10 new churches my first year. We doubled to 20 my second year, and doubled yet again to 40 my third year. Better still, we had laid out the process so those numbers will continue to grow in the future. Yeah God! He granted us success with our impossible assignment.

Solomon's Prayer Regarding His Job

Give Me Wisdom

What do you do when you are faced with having big shoes to fill on your job? How do you replace a larger-than-life legend?

Pray for wisdom. Let me explain.

David had been Israel's real live action superhero of 1000 B.C. He was good looking, dashing, intelligent, hugely talented, and a larger-than-life living legend. He was a man's man and a ladies' man, and yet he was a man after God's own heart. David's résumé reads like a fantasy. He was a boy shepherd, military hero, gifted songwriter, folk legend, national spiritual leader, and king. He had killed Goliath, eluded Saul's army, recruited a band of merry men, become the king, led a tiny nation to become a world power, written many Psalms, created the "Bathsheba-gate" scandal, survived an ugly military coup plotted by his own son, and he planned to build God a great temple.

When David died, the weight of a young nation rested on the untested shoulders of his son, Solomon. He had to step up and take David's place as king. Talk about big shoes to fill!

Yet God knows when we are facing more than we can handle, and He knows just what we need. So God appeared to Solomon in a dream and made him the unconditional proposal: "Ask Me for whatever you want and I will give it to you." To his credit, Solomon knew what to ask for.

On that night God appeared to Solomon, and said to him, "Ask! What shall I give you?" And Solomon said to God: "You have shown great mercy to David my father, and have made me king in his place. Now, O Lord God, let Your promise to David my father be established, for You have made me king over a people like the dust of the earth in multitude. Now **give me wisdom** *and knowledge, that I may go out and come in before this people; for who can judge this great people of Yours?"* (2 Chronicles 1:7-10)

Solomon asked for what he believed to be the most important gift anyone can receive—wisdom. He ranked wisdom ahead of money or looks or miracle powers.

Wisdom, as it is used in the Scriptures, could be best defined as seeing and responding to situations from God's point of view. It is skillful living. It is the combination of good character, high competence, and true Christ-likeness.

Solomon was a diligent student and he used his time growing up in the court of a king to study from the greatest minds of his land. He accumulated the teachings of the ages and collected the parables of the sages. It was his conclusion that the road to blessing leads through the doorway of wisdom. In his book, Proverbs, he wrote the following:

Happy is the man who finds wisdom, and the man who gains understanding; for her proceeds are better than the profits of silver, and her gain than fine gold. She is more precious than rubies, and all the things you may desire cannot compare with her. Length of days is in her right hand, in her left hand riches and honor. Her ways are ways of pleasantness, and all her paths are peace. She is a tree of life to those who take hold of her, and happy are all who retain her (Proverbs 3:13-18).

God liked Solomon's request for wisdom. So He was glad to grant it, and then some.

Then God said to Solomon: "Because this was in your heart, and you have not asked riches or wealth or honor or the life of your enemies, nor have you asked long life—but have asked wisdom and knowledge for yourself, that you may judge My people over whom I have made you king—wisdom and knowledge are granted to you; and I will give you riches and wealth and honor, such as none of the kings have had who were before you, nor shall any after you have the like" (2 Chronicles 1:11-12).

You know the rest of the story. Solomon was later recognized as the world's wisest man (see 1 Kings 4:29-33). The "wisdom" books of the Bible—Proverbs, Song of Solomon, and Ecclesiastes—came from his divinely inspired pen. It was God who answered his prayer for wisdom. Beyond that, God also made him the world's richest man as well.

God's Promise of Wisdom for Those Who Ask

God so loves to give wisdom that He challenges us to pray for it. The aged pastor James wrote:

If any of you lacks wisdom, let him ask of God, who gives to all liberally and without reproach, and it will be given to him (James 1:5).

With what decisions are you currently wrestling? Do you need wisdom to carry out your work more effectively? Do you need insight into a sticky work relationship? Do your job responsibilities require you to make decisions that affect the livelihoods of other people? Are there other areas where you need wisdom?

Ask.

Many times when I have been stumped by a challenging work decision, I have paused to ask for wisdom. I cannot tell you the number of times God has led us to the right decision.

How to Pray for Your Job

Lord, thank You for my work. I ask You to answer these four requests:

+ *Please grant me favor so I can get done the work I need to get done.*

+ *Strengthen my hands. I ask for godly energy, enthusiasm, and endurance to finish off tasks.*

+ *Grant me success today, no matter how big the task or how difficult the assignment.*

+ *Give me wisdom. Help me see and respond to every situation from Your point of view. Give me skill in living. Help me increase in godly character, true competence, and genuine Christ-likeness. Amen.*

Questions for Thought

1. What can we learn from the way Nehemiah did his job that will make *our job* more enjoyable and effective?

2. What can we learn from the prayer of Abraham's servant that will make *our job* more effective?

3. What can we learn from Solomon's prayer as he faced his job that would help us *in our job?*

Section III

Your Daily Challenge

Chapter 9

How to Pray When You Have a Rotten Boss

Dave Earley

*Whoever does not love his work cannot hope that it will
please others.* —Thomas Jefferson (attributed)

*David behaved wisely in all his ways, and the Lord was
with him* (1 Samuel 18:14).

HAVE you ever had to work for a rotten boss? Maybe the boss
you have now is insecure, jealous of you, incompetent, or
even downright abusive. Be encouraged. You aren't the first to have
to deal with a terrible boss. Three thousand years ago, Israel's future
king, David, had the horrible misfortune of working for one of the
worst bosses in history—King Saul.

After bringing deliverance to the Israelis by killing the Philistine giant Goliath, David was on the fast track. The people loved
him, and Saul quickly promoted him. God blessed David as he
went undefeated as a general and his popularity soared. Everything
regarding his job was on its way up. It was almost too good to last...
and it didn't.

DAVID'S BOSS BECAME MURDEROUSLY JEALOUS

After returning from the victory over Goliath, David's popularity grew beyond that of his boss, King Saul. This was too much for Saul to handle. He allowed a seed of bitter resentment to sprout in his heart.

> *Now it had happened as they were coming home, when David was returning from the slaughter of the Philistine, that the women had come out of all the cities of Israel, singing and dancing, to meet King Saul, with tambourines, with joy, and with musical instruments. So the women sang as they danced, and said: "Saul has slain his thousands, and David his ten thousands." Then Saul was very angry, and the saying displeased him; and he said, "They have ascribed to David ten thousands, and to me they have ascribed only thousands. Now what more can he have but the kingdom?" So Saul eyed David from that day forward* (1 Samuel 18:6-9).

Not everyone is pleased when you succeed on your job. Don't be surprised if someone, even your boss, gets jealous.

DAVID'S SPIRITUAL POWER BROUGHT CONVICTION TO HIS BOSS

David's boss, Saul, was insecure and guilty regarding his own fear of Goliath and failure to step up when his nation needed him. Under-confident in his own abilities and in his distant relationship with the Lord, Saul grew murderously paranoid and envious of David.

Saul was clearly a hurting man. Hurting people are the ones who hurt others, and in this case he projected his own pain into hurting David. In an ugly outburst, Saul even tried to kill him with a spear. Being unsuccessful, he sent David off to war to get him out of sight, and to possibly get David killed.

And Saul cast the spear, for he said, "I will pin David to the wall!" But David escaped his presence twice. Now Saul was afraid of David, because the Lord was with him, but had departed from Saul. Therefore Saul removed him from his presence, and made him his captain over a thousand… (1 Samuel 18:11-13).

God often puts us in work environments around people who are trying to run from Him. Those are the very people He has sent us to reach. Often our godly living becomes a source of conviction to them. Don't be surprised if they treat you differently because you are a follower of Jesus.

In Spite of His Boss's Attacks, God Blessed David More

Saul's plan backfired. David was the type of worker God could bless, and He did bless David with more success. As Saul became increasingly mentally disturbed, he withdrew deeper into depression and jealousy. Yet by sending David out, David merely grew in greater popularity with the people. The more David did right, the more his boss hated him.

> *And David behaved wisely in all his ways, and the Lord was with him. Therefore, when Saul saw that he behaved very wisely, he was afraid of him. But all Israel and Judah loved David, because he went out and came in before them* (1 Samuel 18:14-16).

God is often faithful to bless His workers even when, or especially if, their bosses try to make things hard for them. Don't be surprised if things get worse before they get better.

David's Boss Persistently Attacked

David's boss was persistent in his attacks, yet God blessed David even more (see 1 Sam. 18:17-27). Saul's next feeble attempt to hurt David was to send him back to battle in the hopes the Philistines would kill him. Saul then schemed that by allowing his daughter Michal to marry David, he would die trying to raise the bizarre marriage price of the dowry (which was 100 Philistine foreskins). Yet David exceeded Saul's strange request and returned with 200 Philistine foreskins! The more his boss attacked him, the more God blessed David.

David Grew in Popularity and Saul Increased in Jealousy

David's popularity grew even more after David returned with the marriage price, and Saul grew even more insecure. Their relationship began to unravel and disintegrate. At this point, Saul had gone from being David's king, to his boss, to his father-in-law, to becoming David's persistent enemy.

> *Thus Saul saw and knew that the Lord was with David, and that Michal, Saul's daughter, loved him; and Saul was still more afraid of David. So Saul became David's enemy continually* (1 Samuel 18:28-29).

Sadly, despite our best efforts, people in our workplace can choose to become our enemies. There are times when even our bosses can stand against us and become our enemies.

DEALING WITH AN ENEMY

As the Word of God, the Bible is the world's most honest and practical book. It gives us several guidelines for dealing with an enemy.

First, outlive your enemy. Let your attitude and responses continually be above the ordinary. Don't let an enemy's pettiness pull you down to his level. Often the Lord will turn his heart to you as a result of your loving, godly lifestyle. "*When a man's ways please the Lord, he makes even his enemies to be at peace with him*" (Prov. 16:7).

Second, out-serve your enemy. Look for every opportunity you can to help an enemy. Often the Lord uses your servant's heart to win over your enemies.

> *Therefore if your enemy is hungry, feed him; if he is thirsty, give him a drink; for in so doing you will heap coals of fire on his head* (Romans 12:20).

Third, out-love your enemy. Love is a command, not an option. It is a choice, not a feeling. It is a gift that is given, not earned. No matter how badly your boss treats you, you should ask the Lord to love him or her through you. Often an enemy will test you to see if you are genuine. Your active, authentic love may be the only Jesus your enemy will ever see.

> *But I say to you who hear: Love your enemies, do good to those who hate you, bless those who curse you, and pray for those who spitefully use you. To him who strikes you on the one cheek, offer the other also. And from him who takes away your cloak, do not withhold your tunic either. Give to everyone who asks of you. And from him who takes away your goods do not ask them back. And just as you want men to do to you, you also do to them likewise. But if you love those who love you, what credit is that to you? For even sinners love those who love them. And if you do good to those who do good to you, what credit is that to you? For even sinners do the same. And if you lend to those from whom you hope to receive back, what credit is that to you? For even sinners lend to sinners to receive as much back. But love your enemies, do good, and lend, hoping for nothing in return; and your reward will be great, and you will be sons of the Most High, for He is kind to the unthankful and evil* (Luke 6:27-35).

True Christianity is simple, but not easy. Only God can give us the grace to love our enemies. Yet as we obey His commands to do good to our enemies, to bless them and to pray for them, God gives us the grace to keep loving them.

In Spite of It All

In spite of all that his enemies and boss did or tried to do to him, David continued to do his best and behaved wisely.

Then the princes of the Philistines went out to war. And so it was, whenever they went out, that David behaved more wisely than all the servants of Saul, so that his name became highly esteemed (1 Samuel 18:30).

David refused to fight Saul, but instead focused his energy and efforts on doing the best job he could do. Others took note of his excellent behavior and esteemed him for it. Later on, this would pay off for David. The people would remember and crown him king (see 2 Sam. 5:1-5).

It is one thing to do right at the first. It is another thing to do right after our boss continues to treat us badly. Yet, we must call upon God for the strength and grace to continue being our best even when we are treated the worst.

David's Situation Got Even Worse

Even Saul's own son, Jonathan, tried to point out David's innocence, loyalty, and competence to Saul. But Saul still refused to listen (see 1 Sam. 19:4-5). From that point on, Saul's paranoid homicidal attacks on David escalated until David was forced to flee his job, his home, and his wife. Living as a fugitive, David, Israel's champion, Saul's best general, and the king's own son-in-law had to hide in the wilderness from Saul and his army.

Then Saul called all the people together for war, to go down to Keilah to besiege David and his men.... And David stayed in strongholds in the wilderness, and remained in the mountains in the Wilderness of Ziph. Saul sought him every day... (1 Samuel 23:8,14).

Notice those last five words—*Saul sought him every day*. David's trouble from Saul was not a one-time incident, it was a daily reality. It did not last a few days, or even a few weeks, or even a few months. Saul with his army sought him every day for years! Imagine a deranged king and his army chasing you through the wilderness, dogging your every step, waiting for you to make one mistake and leave yourself vulnerable so he can wipe you off the face of the earth. Yet, God in His wisdom knew David needed this tough training in order to prepare David for the rigors of leading the kingdom in the future.

Sometimes, as God is preparing us for greater promotion in the future, He allows us to go through unjust, unforgiving, unkind, unimaginable difficulties on our jobs. Take courage, David made it through and you can as well.

David Treated His Boss With Respect

David treated his boss with great respect even when King Saul did not deserve it. Maybe you are frustrated on your job. You are being treated unjustly. Your supervisor is insecure and is jealous of you. Or your boss is convicted by your Christianity and has begun to persecute you. Or maybe they are letting their own problems drive them to lash out at you. You are not alone. David faced all that and more. His boss, Saul, spent years hunting David trying to kill him.

Remember that David had done nothing to deserve this treatment. He was the model of humility, dependability, and integrity. He had been very successful at his job. Saul should have been proud of him, appreciated his excellent work, and applauded his efforts. Instead, Saul became a paranoid, homicidal maniac.

Finally David has his opportunity to get revenge.

> *Now it happened, when Saul had returned from following the Philistines, that it was told him, saying, "Take note! David is in the Wilderness of En Gedi." Then Saul took three thousand chosen men from all Israel, and went to seek David and his men on the Rocks of the Wild Goats. So he came to the sheepfolds by the road, where there was a cave; and Saul went in to attend to his needs. (David and his men were staying in the recesses of the cave.) Then the men of David said to him, "This is the day of which the Lord said to you, 'Behold, I will deliver your enemy into your hand, that you may do to him as it seems good to you'"* (1 Samuel 24:1-4).

Do you get the amazing irony and opportunity in this picture! Saul has 3,000 men chasing David, but in his mad lust for vengeance, Saul must answer the call of nature. So he finds himself crouching in a cave—but not just any cave. It happened to be the very cave where David and his men were hiding.

This was David's golden opportunity for revenge. All he had to do was sneak up behind Saul in the dark and cut his head off.

Certainly everyone knew how desperately Saul deserved it. David was innocent and Saul was acting like a giant jerk. By now David had become a seasoned warrior. Killing his enemy would be an easy task. Yet David went the extra mile and treated his boss with a measure of respect that his boss did not deserve.

> *And he [David] said to his men, "The Lord forbid that I should do this thing to my master, the Lord's anointed, to stretch out my hand against him, seeing he is the anointed of the Lord." So David restrained his servants with these words, and did not allow them to rise against Saul. And Saul got up from the cave and went on his way. David also arose afterward, went out of the cave, and called out to Saul, saying, "My lord the king!" And when Saul looked behind him, David stooped with his face to the earth, and bowed down* (1 Samuel 24:6-8).

What?! David had Saul right where he wanted him and let him walk away untouched. David not only refused to kill Saul, he bowed down before him!

No wonder David became such a great boss and king later. No wonder his subordinates followed him so loyally. David learned to treat his boss much better than his boss deserved to be treated. He showed the godly trait of forgiving someone who did not deserve it.

Paul later encouraged us to also resist taking vengeance on our enemies.

> *Repay no one evil for evil. Have regard for good things in the sight of all men. If it is possible, as much as depends on you, live peaceably with all men. Beloved, do not avenge yourselves, but*

rather give place to wrath; for it is written, "Vengeance is Mine, I will repay," says the Lord. Therefore if your enemy is hungry, feed him; if he is thirsty, give him a drink; for in so doing you will heap coals of fire on his head. Do not be overcome by evil, but overcome evil with good (Romans 12:17-21).

David behaved with incredible integrity and treated his evil, disloyal boss with amazing respect and loyalty. As a result, Saul finally saw the light and softened his stance toward David.

...Saul lifted up his voice and wept. Then he said to David: "You are more righteous than I; for you have rewarded me with good, whereas I have rewarded you with evil. And you have shown this day how you have dealt well with me; for when the Lord delivered me into your hand, you did not kill me. For if a man finds his enemy, will he let him get away safely? Therefore may the Lord reward you with good for what you have done to me this day. And now I know indeed that you shall surely be king, and that the kingdom of Israel shall be established in your hand." ...And Saul went home... (1 Samuel 24:16-22).

If Saul can change, your boss can change. Don't quit. Your excellent work ethic, competent abilities, hard-earned skills, respectful attitudes, active love, and fervent prayers are frequently used by God to wear down your worst enemies.

HOW TO PRAY FOR YOUR ROTTEN BOSS

Lord, help me to realize that as long as I live on this earth, I will face difficult and damaging people. Enable me to be an excellent worker regardless of how rotten my human boss may be. Use me to live such a life of spiritual power that it brings conviction on my co-workers. Help me treat my boss with great respect, even when he or she does not deserve it. Give me the grace to actively love and pray for my enemies. Remind me that usually hurting people are those who hurt others. O Lord, help me leave the judgment and vengeance to You. Amen.

QUESTIONS FOR THOUGHT

1. What are some of the purposes why God allows us to have a rotten boss?

2. How and what should you pray about a rotten boss?

3. What should you do when a rotten boss produces profits for the company's bottom line?

4. Is there ever a time when you should go to the next level supervisor above your rotten boss? When is that time, and what are the circumstances?

5. What can you learn about being a "follower of Christ" when you have a rotten boss?

6. What can you do to make a good boss out of a rotten boss, and how would you go about it?

Chapter 10

How to Pray for Your Witness on the Job

Elmer Towns

I long to accomplish great and noble tasks, but it is my chief duty to accomplish humble tasks as though they were great and noble. The world is moved along not only by the mighty shoves of its heroes, but also by the aggregate of the tiny pushes of each honest worker. —Helen Keller

…you shall be witnesses to Me… (Acts 1:8).

JESUS told us to be witnesses to Him everywhere: *"Jerusalem, and in all Judea and Samaria, and to the end of the earth"* (Acts 1:8). If Jesus meant everywhere—and He did—then that includes our workplace because we have a physical location where we work at our jobs.

This chapter deals with three aspects of witnessing:

+ First, we must pray about our preparation to witness.

+ Second, we must pray for those to whom we witness.

+ Third, we must pray about the actual witness itself— how we present Christ to people on the job.

First—Pray to be Prepared

Pray for your preparation to witness, and ask God to make you a good testimony.

Many have said that God is more concerned about what you *become* for Him than He is about what you *do* for Him. That is probably an overstatement, but it does have some truth. Before you can witness for God you must have something to share with others. Therefore, biblical evangelism is more than an activity; it grows out of a walk with Christ. The verbal witness can be no more effective than the lifestyle witness.

Someone said, "The way you walk makes so much noise that I cannot hear what you say." Obviously, a godly life will not always guarantee a fair hearing for verbal testimony, but anything less than a godly life is sure to drown out even the best verbal testimony.

Evangelism has long been thought of as an act of reaping souls, actually leading someone to Christ. The emphasis has been placed upon picking ripe fruit. That approach works well where the orchards have already been planted, watered, fertilized, trimmed, and nurtured. In this case, evangelism is thought of as an activity, or actually getting a lost person to pray to receive Christ.

Lifestyle evangelism is a process of living the gospel so unsaved people can see Christ in you. It is planting the seed of the gospel, watering it, fertilizing it, and finally harvesting it.

We can no longer assume that people in the United States know the gospel, because we can no longer assume America is a Christian nation. Most unsaved Americans do not know the gospel because they are blinded spiritually. Also school, media, entertainment, and probably all culture is not inclined to God. Since the gospel is a dynamic message, the unsaved do not understand it by merely knowing the verbiage—the words that make up the gospel. The unsaved must *see* the words of the gospel in our lives to understand its meaning. Hence the phrase, lifestyle evangelism.

While explaining the claims of the gospel verbally, you must demonstrate the effectiveness of those claims through your life. Paul reminded the Thessalonian believers that he and Silas had not only proclaimed the gospel to them, but they had also demonstrated its effectiveness in their own lives (see 1 Thess. 1:5). Commenting about his witness, Paul said, "*What manner of entering in we had unto you, and how ye turned to God from idols to serve the living and true God*" (1 Thess. 1:9 KJV).

Lifestyle evangelism doesn't begin by telling someone about Jesus, it begins with our godly lifestyle that makes people want the Savior that we have.

A person is never saved by merely knowing the words of the Bible or understanding Christian doctrine. Eternal life is in Jesus Christ, and a person must receive Him to become a Christian and have eternal life (see John 1:12). Many in our secular society think Christianity is only a system of beliefs. It is that, but it's based upon the new life we receive when we were saved. Jesus said, "*I have come that they may have life, and that they may have it more abundantly*" (John 10:10). Therefore, lifestyle evangelism communicates Christianity from life to life, your lifestyle communicates the life of Christ to your business friends.

Not all people at your place of work are equally receptive to you or to the gospel.

Some you will not reach because they will reject you, they have difficulty with your position, your personality, or many other reasons. Others have had a bad encounter with a Christian; or perhaps for their liberal orientation, they have rejected the gospel because of its personal ramifications. They may not like your stand on abortion, drinking alcohol, free sex, marriage, the family, etc. So remember, there are many associates who you will have difficulty reaching; but do not be discouraged, God does unusual things.

There are always some associates you can reach more effectively than others; perhaps those who already know and trust you. These will listen to a witness for Jesus Christ. Therefore, think through all your friends and associates, evaluate those who are open to you, and those who are not responsive. Those who are most open, give them more priority of your prayer and effort.

In the parable of the sower (the sower of seed was a Christian witness), the seed (the gospel) fell on four different kinds of soil (see Matt. 13:1-9;18-23). The first soil was the path next to the field which was hard and packed down. When the seed was sown, birds came and ate it up. This represents people who are hardened to the gospel. When you say something Christian to them, it may have no impact on them.

The second soil was the rocky places that had a little depth of earth. When the seed was sown, it sprang up immediately but when the sun and wind came, the seed died. These represent people who may listen eagerly the first time we talk to them, but in the long run, they will not respond to Jesus Christ.

The third was the seed sown among the thorns, represented by the lust, sin, and the attractions of the world. Some people at work will not listen because of their love for worldly amusements.

The fourth was the good soil, and each of those gave forth different quantities of harvest. So from your witness you never know what God will do.

Lord, help me see the spiritual temperature in all of the people with whom I work. Help me understand each one and give me wisdom to influence them at their level of receptivity. Help me win someone to salvation. Amen.

Second — Pray for Them

Pray for those to whom you witness. You can influence those with whom you repeatedly and systematically come into contact, but have no close personal relationship with them. These people represent the largest group of prospects that you will meet every day.

While there are many difficulties in forming a relationship with people with a view of witnessing for Jesus Christ, there are biblical examples that clearly illustrate that they can be reached for Christ. You can influence those who work with you and your superiors. You can make friends with them, and win them to Christ.

However, reaching business associates will not just happen. You have to be intentional. You must pray about it, you must work at it, and there's no better way than to start where you are with the people who are closest around you.

Make a prayer list of those with whom you work, including your superiors and those who work for you. Bring their names daily before the Father, asking for the following that:

1. God will prepare their hearts.

2. God will give you wisdom about how to reach out to them.

3. When a witnessing opportunity arises, you will know what to say.

4. God will give you opportunities to present the gospel.

5. God will work out circumstances where you can be a better friend to them.

Lord, I pray for opportunities to witness for You on the job. When they open up, give me wisdom to say the correct thing in the correct way that will influence them toward salvation. Amen.

Third—Pray About Your Witness

Pray about your actual witness. You are employed to perform a specific function at work, your main purpose is not to be a personal soul winner. However, everyone has different levels of attention and/or concentration at the workplace. And part of the attention at the workplace involves establishing relationships with your fellow workers. Why? Because most places you work as a team, there is a team leader, associates who will help you complete your job, and there are those under you to whom you give direction and work orders. The following circle will help you to think through your various relationships on the job.

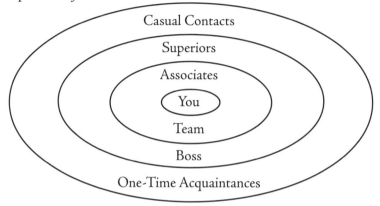

Reaching Out to Work Associates

As Jesus walked from the city of Capernaum, He saw a man named Matthew sitting at his tax collector's booth. "Follow Me," Jesus said to him (see Luke 5:27-29). So Matthew got up and followed Him. Because of that encounter, Matthew's life was completely changed:

Later, Matthew invited Jesus and His disciples to his home as dinner guests, along with many tax collectors and other disreputable sinners. But when the Pharisees saw this, they asked His disciples, "Why does your Teacher eat with such scum?" When Jesus heard this, He said, "Healthy people don't need a doctor—sick people do." Then He added: "Now go and learn the meaning of this Scripture: 'I want you to show mercy, not offer sacrifices. For I have come to call not those who think they are righteous, but those who know they are sinners'" (Matthew 9:10-13 NLT).

Obviously from the Scriptures we realize that tax collectors were shunned by the general public because they were notoriously wicked. The Roman government determined how much taxes they wanted from each person, and employed tax collectors to get this money. The tax collector added his commission, which many times was oppressive and unjust. When people complained, the tax collector used Roman soldiers to exact the taxes. Because of that, tax collectors were considered a dishonorable profession of the day.

As a result, Matthew may not have had a large number of close, personal friends in the city of Capernaum where he lived. However, Matthew probably knew a number of associates or co-workers who worked for Rome. These are the ones he reached with the message of salvation. These are the ones to whom Matthew witnessed.

Matthew responded when Jesus called him to abandon his profession and become His disciple. It was only natural for Matthew to reach out to those who worked with him and for him. How did he do it? The Gospel of Luke records that Matthew *"gave Him a great feast in his own house. And there were a great number of tax collectors and others who sat down with them"* (Luke 5:29).

Matthew reached out to those who were his equals and those who worked for him. He probably never considered the impossible criticism from the religious community for his witness.

Notice how Matthew reached out to those who worked with him:

1. He did not let any criticism of his friends stop him.

2. He did not attempt to maintain a separation between his personal and professional life.

3. He used his relationships with his fellow workers to introduce them to Christ.

4. He found a common interest to present Christ— sharing a meal, eating.

5. He opened up his home and family to his work associates.

It probably sounds very simplistic, but eating is always a good place to maintain a relationship. Eating is something everybody has to do, and everybody wants to do. Anyone can take an associate to lunch with the desire to witness for Jesus Christ. Pray about it, and plan to do it.

Lord, I will try to reach with the gospel the people I work around. Give me a heart of concern for them and give me wisdom to know how to do it. Amen.

Witnessing to Superiors

There's one place in Scripture when Paul witnessed to a Philippian jailer (see Acts 16:25-34). He was not witnessing on a horizontal plane, but talking to someone who was his unquestioned superior. Paul had been arrested and placed in prison; the jailer was in charge of seeing that the cell block was kept secure. Therefore Paul and the Philippian jailer were not on an equal basis; Paul definitely had fewer privileges.

Around midnight Paul and Silas were praying and singing hymns to God, and the other prisoners were listening. Suddenly, there was a massive earthquake, and the prison was shaken to its foundations. All the doors immediately flew open, and the chains of every prisoner fell off! The jailer woke up to see the prison doors wide open. He assumed the prisoners had escaped, so he drew his sword to kill himself. But Paul shouted to him, "Stop! Don't kill yourself! We are all here!" The jailer called for lights and ran to the dungeon and fell down trembling before Paul and Silas. Then he brought them out and asked, "Sirs, what must I do to be saved?" They replied, "Believe in the Lord Jesus and you will be saved, along with everyone in your household" (Acts 16:25-31 NLT).

What is not said in the Scriptures is that Paul probably had such a quiet attitude as a prisoner, that the jailer knew he was a Christian. It could have been Paul's meekness, or his lack of retaliation, or his lack of anger, or just his general submissive attitude; but in any case, the jailer knew that Paul was different.

Probably the charges against Paul were known by the jailer, that he had been preaching Jesus Christ in the city of Philippi. Also, Paul had cast the demon out of a young slave girl that infuriated her owners. They used the slave girl to predict the future and when the demon was gone, they lost their business edge. This was the crisis that caused Paul's arrest. The jailer probably knew all of this.

So when God sent the earthquake, it was only natural for the jailer to react in panic. Because he was trusted to keep the prisoners, and he assumed they had escaped, he planned to kill himself.

The jailer was shocked that no one escaped when they had the opportunity. It was then that he asked the question, *"What must I do to be saved?"* (Acts 16:30).

There's a lesson here. If you live a Christian lifestyle before your associates at work and as consistently to those above you, there will come a crisis when you will have an opportunity to witness for Jesus Christ. Therefore:

1. Pray for your witness.

2. Live consistently.

3. Be ready to speak when the crisis comes, because everyone has some type of crisis in their lives.

What happened after the Philippian jailer believed in Christ?

Then they [Paul and Silas] *shared the Word of the Lord with him* [the jailer] *and all who lived in his household. That same hour the jailer washed their wounds and he and everyone in his household were immediately baptized. Then he brought them into his house and set a meal before them. He and his entire household rejoiced because they had all believed in God* (Acts 16:32-34 ELT).

This was probably not the only time when Paul built a Christian relationship with prison guards. Later Paul wrote a letter to the Philippians and included in the letter his jail experience in Rome. It was a letter that the Philippian church could identify with, because their church had started from a jail experience. Paul wrote:

And I want you to know, my dear brothers and sisters that everything that has happened to me here has helped to spread the Good News. For everyone here, including the whole palace guard knows that I am in chains because of Christ. And because of my imprisonment, most of the believers here have gained confidence and boldly speak God's message without fear (Philippians 1:12-14 NLT).

The guards were probably rotated from one assignment to another, and probably included both prison and the palace. Because of the strong witness of Paul, when the guards got into the palace, they witnessed to Caesar's household. So Paul later writes: *"All the other Christians send their greetings too, especially those who work in Caesar's palace"* (Phil. 4:22 ELT).

We did not know who it was in Caesar's palace who got saved, whether these were workers or members of Caesar's family, but it's apparent that someone touched their lives for Christ.

What can we learn from this illustration? The people you influence at your job can in turn influence people you will never meet in life. So it's possible to be a good witness to those who are your superiors and that influence go all the way up the line to the owner. Retain your integrity at work so your reputation will penetrate the boss's office and the board room.

But this means more than just talking about Christ. You must also be a good testimony of hard work, diligent work, and smart work. You must work well and be productive for the company. Paul says: *"Be not weary in well-doing"* (2 Thess. 3:13 KJV).

The Living Bible translates the phrase "well-doing":

*So don't get tired of doing what is good. Don't get discouraged
and give up, for we will reap a harvest of blessing at the appropriate time* (Galatians 6:9 TLB).

*Lord, help me be a good witness of my faith to my superiors.
May my work please them so they will listen to the gospel when
I share it. Use me to win some of my superiors to Jesus Christ.
Amen.*

WITNESSING TO CASUAL OR ONE-TIME ACQUAINTANCES

When you witness to someone you see on a one-time basis, it's
entirely different from witnessing to someone you work with every
day. If it's a one-time experience, be sensitive to God's leading. Pray
for that person as you meet him or her. Say only what you can say.
Then leave the results to God. Witnessing to a complete stranger
involves certain types of relationships whereas witnessing to someone you see day in and day out involves your complete lifestyle.

There will be many people who you slightly touch in your work
experience. This may be someone who delivers a package to your
office or work station, someone who is sent with a message to your
department, or perhaps just a one-time approach from a salesperson.
Probably you can't stop and give the presentation of the gospel on
these occasions. However, you can always be cheerful and friendly.
You never know what a cheerful, friendly word can do.

My wife and I had the occasion to visit a business establish-
ment, and we were rudely received by the receptionist. She criticized

Liberty University where I teach, saying, "You people from Liberty always want an exception...." Liberty University is known for its Christian testimony, and apparently she had an unpleasant encounter with someone from Liberty. I said to my wife, "I'm going to make her my friend."

All I did was to be concerned about her and her job. I told her how difficult it was to deal with so many different kinds of people from the general public. As we were waiting, she had to carry some boxes into the inner office. I jumped up and held the door for her, offering to help carry the boxes. When she let me help her, the whole expression on her face changed. By being friendly, I made a friend.

Jesus met the woman of Samaria by Jacob's Well (see John 4:6-39). And all He asked from her was "a drink of water." That friendly request opened up a conversation, and she told Jesus her life story. Then she went back into the city and told the men all that Jesus had said to her.

This was a woman who had been married five times and was living with a man to whom she was not married. Her association with the men of the city was undoubtedly limited. Yet, when she went back into the city, she formed a bridge with them so that many Samaritans from the village believed in Jesus because the woman had said: *"He told me everything I did"* (John 4:29 ELT).

When the men of the city came out to see Jesus, they begged Him to stay at their village. So He stayed two days, long enough for many of them to hear His message and believe. Then they said to the woman: *"Now we believe because we have heard Him ourselves, not just because of what you told us. He is indeed the Savior of the world"* (John 4:42 TLB).

Lord, I come in contact with many people each day. Help me be a good testimony to all I meet. Then give me an opportunity to share with some the message of salvation. Lord, use me on my job. Amen.

OBSTACLES TO WITNESSING FOR CHRIST AT WORK

Some Christians fail to build a witnessing type relationship with people at work because they're afraid of being misunderstood. They don't want to become a "fanatic" who always presses for decision, or one who brings up salvation in every conversation. Because they're afraid of being misunderstood, they never talk about Christ.

A second obstacle is the natural barrier between a worker and superior. Perhaps you won't witness to them because you're afraid that they may retaliate, like give you a poor job evaluation, or even fire you.

Sometimes people don't build their relationship at work because it's time consuming. They don't want to be drawn away from their focus on their job, or they don't want to be drawn away from their friends outside of the job. Making good witnessing relationships requires dedication and hard work. Remember, friends are not found, they are made.

Some people just think it's best to make a complete separation between their personal life and their work. Since the people at work are identified with their job or profession, therefore they separate from them naturally. Consequently, any attempt to witness for Christ has to overcome that natural barrier between private life and personal life.

You could witness for Christ by simply taking time with people. There are coffee breaks, lunch dates, or other times at work when people are standing around waiting for the next requirement. It takes time to discover people's interests, rather than focusing only on your own. There are natural times when you will lend someone a helping hand, and at the appropriate time you can bring up your faith naturally.

How do you get to know a work associate better? Cultivate interest. Find out what you have in common, do things together. Invite your associate out to lunch, get together for sports or entertainment events, or any other time that's natural for work associates to get together.

Make yourself available in times of hurt or special need. The people at work may have a death in the family, financial reversals, or other serious problems. Sympathize with them, and be there to listen.

Wrap Up

Remember, you must start by *being* a witness before you share a verbal witness. That means your life testimony will probably have a longer lasting positive influence than the words you share. Just being a Christian is never enough.

The old farmer said, "What's in the well, comes up in the bucket," so what is in the heart will come out of the mouth. If you are a good Christian testimony, then you will give a good verbal testimony.

Lord, use me at my job. I want to be a good, living Christian testimony. So show me where I fall short, forgive me of any sin that has hurt my testimony. Give me strength to live for You at work.

Then, Lord, I pray for Your conviction in the hearts of my co-workers and those over me. Work in their hearts to bring them to faith in Christ. Use my life and witness to move them to Christ.

I pray for other Christians where I work. Use them to advance Your Kingdom. May we work together to bring Christ into our workplace. In Christ. Amen.

QUESTIONS FOR THOUGHT

1. How can one be a testimony for Christ when it's not possible to give a verbal witness on the job?

2. How can you respond when another Christian on the job is a "good verbal witness" but a "lousy worker?"

3. What are some of the things for which you should pray when you want to witness for Christ on the job?

4. Do you have a list of co-workers for whom you pray? Who should you add to that list? What do you ask God to do for them?

5. Have you ever asked God to use your Christian witness at work? Could you ask God to "anoint" your witnessing to make a difference in their lives?

Chapter 11

How to Pray for God's Blessing on Your Job

Elmer Towns

We make a living by what we get, but we make a life by what we give. —Winston Churchill

Blessed shall be the…produce of your ground and the increase of your herds…the increase of your cattle and the offspring of your flocks. Blessed shall be your basket and your kneading bowl (Deuteronomy 28:4-5).

SOMETIMES you might pray, "God, bless me at work today." What do you mean by the blessing of God on your work?

Technically, there are four ways to ask God to bless your work or job. First, you ask God to bless you personally—your attitude, your walk with Christ, and all that you are. Second, you ask God to bless the tasks you are doing, that you may be effective and efficient to get a lot done. Third, you ask God to bless the business you work for, or the company where you have a job, that it may prosper and that you may help it have a better bottom line. Fourth, you ask God to bless the product you make, whether it is something mechanical or the service you provide, that you will change lives for the better as an assembly line worker, teacher, counselor, healthcare provider, manager, or whatever position the Lord has provided for you.

Now let's ask another question. What do you mean by the word *bless?* The first time the word *bless* (*barakh*) is found in Scripture suggests its meaning, *"And God blessed them, saying, 'Be fruitful and multiply...'"* (Gen. 1:22). This means God blessed the creation of life by giving it energy, the ability to reproduce, and making it useful for a good purpose.

So the word *bless* means to add value to something, to make it profitable, valuable, or worth something. So when you pray for God to bless your job, you are asking Him to add value to the task you do.

In another case, Rebecca's relatives gave her finances (jewels, clothes, family crest) when the Bible said her relatives "blessed Rebecca," and said to her, *"Our sister, may you become the mother of thousands of ten thousands"* (Gen. 24:60). This blessing is more than giving her a "letter of reference." They were adding value to her life, both financially and spiritually.

Later Esau asked his father, *"Have you not reserved a blessing for me?"* (Gen. 27:36). Here Esau was asking for some additional financial inheritance, because his brother Jacob had stolen the original inheritance from him. Technically the blessing in this situation was a double portion of the family inheritance upon Isaac's death.

This financial value that's added is also seen in Proverbs 10:22, *"The blessing of the Lord makes one rich."*

When you pray for God to bless you at work, or to bless your business, or to bless your productivity, you are asking God to add His value to the things you do at the job. So, we use the phrase "added value" to explain what is meant by "blessing." When you say,

"God bless you," you are saying may God add value to your life and/ or job. Note the following:

> *Blessed shall you be in the city, and blessed shall you be in the country. Blessed shall be the fruit of your body, the produce of your ground, and the increase of your herds…. Blessed shall be your basket and your kneading bowl. The Lord will open to you His good treasure, the heavens, to give the rain to your land in its seasons, and to bless all the work of your hand…* (Deuteronomy 28:3-5,12).

Usually, there is nothing miraculous about the blessing of God on your work. A blessing is not a miracle, inasmuch as a miracle is God's intervention in the laws of nature for a divine purpose. The blessing of God is not His intervention of laws, but rather God working through details to make the things you do more valuable to you, to your boss, to your company, and to the people who use the products or services of the company where you work.

> *Lord, I pray for You to add value to my life as I work, and help me add value to my work team. May my company be blessed, and I pray for You to use the product or services I produce to add value to others. Amen.*

Not a Blessing

When a golfer suffers a heat stroke that leads to a heart attack, he doesn't need the blessing of God, he needs the prayer of healing and a miracle. He needs an ambulance and a hospital.

A man starving to death does not need God to bless him; he needs food. When he receives something to eat, he usually "gobbles" it down, not thinking of its taste. The food saves his life. What's more than a blessing?

- A blessing is good, but a miraculous intervention is much more than a blessing.

- A blessing is God's prosperity, but a supernatural deliverance from trouble is much more than a blessing.

- A blessing makes your life more enjoyable, but when God solves a problem, it is much more than a blessing.

- A blessing makes you effective, but deliverance from addiction is much more than a blessing.

When God blesses your job, He doesn't necessarily intervene in the laws of nature, nor does He supernaturally deliver you from trouble on the job, nor does He deliver you from addiction, or from any other supernatural intervention by God. Rather, the blessing of God can be what follows.

When God blesses your job, He makes it enjoyable, so that you are happy in your work environment and you look forward to going to work.

When God blesses your job, He makes you work with energy and efficiency so that you do a better job.

When God blesses your job, you are filled with new determination to learn, grow, and get better at your job.

When God blesses your job, He simply gives you His presence at work so that you are more happy and peaceful as you work that day.

When God blesses your job, you have a better working relationship with your team so that you enjoy your job and they enjoy you.

When God blesses your job, He helps you to make someone else's life happier, easier, or prosperous.

When God blesses your job, He uses you in lifestyle evangelism so others see Christ has possessed you, and that your work brings glory to Jesus Christ, and as a result some are brought to salvation.

When God blesses your job, you are refreshed and revitalized so that the job does not suck all of the life out of you, but rather you give happiness to others at work, while you fulfill the job for which you are employed.

Lord, Your blessing makes me useful and happy; I ask for it and by faith I receive it from You. Bless me today at my job. Amen.

How God Blesses

Early in the morning I eat a bowl of cereal and milk; it's my normal breakfast. The food doesn't save my life, nor is it miraculous intervention; it sustains my life. But my wife cuts a few strawberries into my cereal. Now that's a blessing. She adds enjoyment and taste.

When you pray for a blessing at work, you might be praying for God to work through small details to get the job done. As mentioned previously, remember, the world says, "the devil is in the details," but the Christian realizes that "God is in the details." God adds value to your work by making you more efficient and effective.

When I meet God early in the morning to worship, pray, or learn from the Word of God, God blesses my life with His presence. I get added value for the day.

But perhaps our greatest added value is God's presence when He blesses us with Himself. The New Testament word for "blessing" is *eulogia*. The word *logia* is to speak. Note the term, "The cup of blessing" in First Corinthians 10:16. This is a technical term from Jewish liturgy signifying the cup upon which a blessing was pronounced. God can bless many things.

When you ask God to bless your job, it is possible that you in turn can bless God because of your job. The old servant who was sent on the task by Abraham to find a wife for Isaac said, *"I bowed my head and worshiped the Lord, and blessed the Lord God of my master Abraham…"* (Gen. 24:48). Here the servant is adding value to God, meaning he's worshiping, exalting, and praising God for helping him get the job done.

Therefore, when you ask God to bless your job, and He does, you must then turn around and bless God for answering your prayer.

PRAYING BEFORE YOU GO TO WORK

Obviously when you pray for your job, you are going to pray for four things. First, you are going to pray that you do an excellent job to please your superiors. Second, you're going to pray that your life enhances (blesses) the lives of those you work around, your work team. Third, you're going to pray that God blesses the company where you work so that it becomes financially healthy and that the company has a good bottom line. Fourth, you are going to pray that God uses the product or service that comes from your work, so that those who buy your product or receive your service get added value to their lives.

THE FIVE LAWS OF GOD'S BLESSING

Law 1:   God wants to bless people.

Law 2:   God uses people to bless people.

Law 3:   God's people must be blessed before they can bless others.

Law 4:   To bless others, we must follow God's pattern.

Law 5:   Those who are blessed experience improved lives.

LAW 1: GOD WANTS TO BLESS PEOPLE

Some people picture God as an old man standing in Heaven hoarding His money. They think He makes up strict rules just to make people miserable. However, that's not the God of the Bible. God loves all people and wants to add value to their lives. That may be money, but it's not always money. Sometimes God blesses the way you work, or the productivity of your work. Sometimes God's blessing is God's happiness that makes life more valuable. Obviously the best added value of all is when they experience His presence in their lives.

Think for a moment about money, God loves to bless people with money. He wants them to enjoy wealth. But He blesses them with money for a purpose. God wants you to bless your church or His work with a financial gift. Or God may want to send revival to your heart. God will bless people when they follow His formula for money:

> Bring all the tithes into the storehouse...and try Me...if I will not open for you the windows of heaven and pour out for you such blessing (Malachi 3:10).

God's plan is "to give in order to get." You can receive God's blessings in your life when you deal with the opposite—selfishness. "Give, and it will be given to you" (Luke 6:38). So, we give our tithes and offerings to God as we attend church each Sunday. In return, God adds value to our lives and to the lives of our family. But the added value is not always money. Sometimes it's inner peace, sometimes it's satisfaction.

Sometimes the blessing of God is good health when God protects us from germs and bacteria. Sometimes the blessing of God is physical strength that comes through our food so we can get our work done, play a sport, exercise, or get involved in more church activities. At other times the blessing of God may be physical stamina, He gives us a great desire to work harder, succeed at work, or to live life to the fullest.

Sometimes the blessing of God is long life. Notice the promise of Scripture, God will bless us to see our grandchildren.

The Lord bless you out of Zion, and may you see the good of Jerusalem all the days of your life. Yes, may you see your children's children... (Psalm 128:5-6).

Also pray for the blessing of a happy countenance. Have you ever realized that your life is a billboard that tells others what's going on on the inside? When we are discouraged, it shows on our faces. The same with happiness, there's a bright, attractive smile.

Law 2: God Uses His People to Bless Others

Anyone can be a blessing to others, no matter who you are, or where you are. It doesn't depend on your age, your skill, or your maturity in faith. You can bless your friends.

When Abraham came back from battle, he shared some of the spoils of war, which were the treasures he got from defeating an enemy. He gave some of his money to Melchizedek, who at that time blessed Abraham saying:

Blessed be Abram of God Most High, possessor of heaven and earth; and blessed be God Most High, who has delivered your enemies into your hand (Genesis 14:19-20).

Just as Melchizedek blessed his friend Abraham, sometimes you may bless a friend at work by helping him make a sale and helping her get a financial commission or a bonus.

Remember that fathers can bless their children. Fathers add value to your children just as when, *"By faith Isaac blessed Jacob..."*

(Heb. 11:20). Isaac prayed that Jacob would inherit his own legacy, which was tied to both finances and spiritual leadership.

Parents can add value to their children by naturally blessing them with physical things, or spiritually blessing them with the riches of God, or by blessing them to prepare for their life's work.

Remember this section discusses God using people to bless others. The Old Testament priests were commanded, *"You shall bless the children of Israel"* (Num. 6:23), saying:

> *The Lord bless you and keep you; the Lord make His face shine upon you, and be gracious to you; the Lord lift up His countenance upon you, and give you peace* (Numbers 6:24-26).

When a minister blesses the congregation by speaking a blessing into their lives at a benediction, what is he doing? He is speaking the Lord's presence into the lives of His people. If they are willing to receive the blessing of God, their lives can be uplifted and God can add value to them.

Law 3: God's People Must Be Blessed Before They Can Bless Others

It's a basic law of life, selfish people don't have strength or enjoyment to give to others. They are like vacuums, sucking everything into their own webs. They are like black holes in space, pulling everything near them into their own orbits. Black holes have tremendous heat, because everything sucked into them is immediately burned up. Then what happens? Eventually a black hole implodes upon itself. Is this not a description of selfish people? Don't most selfish people eventually implode upon themselves?

The problem with selfish people is that they don't encourage others, they don't give time to others, nor do they give finances to others. Since life is enriched by relationships, selfish people miss that enrichment.

The more blessings you give to others at work, the stronger you become. So learn to bless others, and in the process you will bless yourself. When you add value to others by helping to solve a problem, or explaining something, you have added value to both others and yourself.

You can't give to others what you haven't experienced. Life is like the measles, you have to have measles to pass them on. In the same way, you must be able to drive a car before you can teach your children how to do it. And you must be able to play golf before you can give others instruction in the game.

When Jacob ran away from home, he went to work for his uncle, Laban, some 800 miles away from father and mother. Apparently in spite of all his character flaws, Jacob was at least a hard worker. So what did the uncle testify? *"...I have learned by experience that the Lord has blessed me for your sake"* (Gen. 30:27).

God had promised to bless Jacob (see Gen. 28:3) and as God blessed Jacob, that blessing flowed into the life of his uncle Laban.

What blessing have you spilled into the life of others? As you pray for them, encourage them, and help them through their work difficulties, you can bless other people.

LAW 4: TO BLESS OTHERS, WE MUST FOLLOW GOD'S PATTERN

Blessing is usually tied to speaking. When the priest blessed the congregation, God said, *"So they shall put My name on the children of Israel, and I will bless them"* (Num. 6:27). So if you tell somebody at work, "God bless you," make sure you are pointing them to Jesus, and not relying on some empty words.

Believe What You Say

When you want to bless someone, trust God to fulfill it through your spoken word and actions. Notice what God said about Isaac, *"By faith Isaac blessed Jacob…"* (Heb. 11:20).

Since *giving* a blessing is tied to faith, we should not be surprised that *receiving* a blessing is also tied to faith. Notice what God promised:

Now it shall come to pass, if you diligently obey the voice of the Lord your God, to observe carefully all His commandments which I command you today, that the Lord your God will set you high above all nations of the earth. And all these blessings shall come upon you and overtake you, because you obey the voice of the Lord your God (Deuteronomy 28:1-2).

Use the Bible in Blessing

When you're speaking God's Word into people's lives, make sure they not only hear the Bible, but that they also understand what it means. God has promised, *"Blessed is he who reads and those who hear the words of this prophecy, and keep those things which are written in it…*" (Rev. 1:3). So people can either read the Bible or hear the Bible, but they must understand the Bible to have the blessing of God.

Why will God use His Word to bless the life of a co-worker? Because *"the Word of God is alive and powerful"* (Heb. 4:12 NLT). So when you use the Word of God properly, it will change the lives of your co-workers.

Remember, you may share God's Word with people at work, but God does not give you some special power to bless other people. The blessing comes directly from God to the person you bless.

Every person has immediate and direct access to God. You are not anyone's mediator. Rather, *"there is one God and one Mediator between God and men, the Man Christ Jesus"* (1 Tim. 2:5).

This does not mean you'll never be used of God to bless other people. Sometimes you may give other people your time or loan them money. Sometimes you might help solve a problem, or show them how to get a job done. God can use you to bless other people, but the blessing comes from God. He is the Blesser, the recipients are the blessees. You are just a servant of God.

Law 5: Those Who Are Blessed Experience Improved Lives

Joseph had ten older brothers who hated him. Of course Joseph brought a lot of the hatred upon himself when he bragged to his older brothers, and they hated him for it. His father, Jacob, gave him the coat of many colors, which symbolized that Joseph was the foreman or overseer on the job; so his brothers hated him and sold him into Egypt as a slave.

Joseph ended up in Potiphar's house as a slave. But notice what happened, *"The Lord blessed the Egyptian's house for Joseph's sake and the blessing of the Lord was on all that he had in the house and in the field"* (Gen. 39:5). This blessing on Joseph's life overflowed to his boss.

That may mean that when God blesses you, you become extremely productive and the place where you work gets richer because of you. You ought to pray constantly that you increase the bottom line of the place where you work. That's also called job security.

It wasn't just that Joseph was honest, trustworthy, and worked hard, he had the added value of God's presence in his life. So as a result, Potiphar had financial rewards because of one slave—Joseph.

But it just wasn't the workers who were blessed of God. God also blesses owners and bosses. Boaz owned fields and hired many people to harvest his crops. In addition to that, he allowed the poor to glean his fields after his workers had harvested the crops. The workers recognized God's blessing on Boaz because they said, *"The Lord bless you!"* (Ruth 2:4). As a result, Boaz was a man of great wealth (see Ruth 2:1).

There was another boss who had experienced a financial blessing because God's hand was on him. The Lord *"blessed the work of his [Job's] hands"* (Job 1:10). That means Job became very wealthy by working with his hands. As a result, he gained houses (probably helping to build them), flocks and herds (helping to actually deliver the newborn to his cattle), and fields (probably working with his hands to plant and harvest crops).

Why did God bless Job? *"Job was blameless and upright, and one who feared God and shunned evil"* (Job 1:1). God blessed Job because of his character and spirituality. As a result of God's blessing on Job, God put a hedge of protection about him. Job had a *"hedge around him, around his household, and around all that he has on every side"* (Job 1:10).

A hedge of protection at your work means God protects you from making errors, from unjust accusations, gossip, and those who would try to stab you in the back—betray you.

What can you do about gossip, backbiting, and those who would betray you? The Bible tells you to pray for spiritual protection, *"lead us into temptation, but deliver us from the evil one"* (Matt. 6:13). Beyond that, God says, *"Bless those who curse you, and pray for those who spitefully use you"* (Luke 6:28). Not only can you pray that they would understand the blessing of God, but you can also pray that they would be convicted of their sin and have a desire for God's blessing in their lives and your life. When rumors and scoffers try to ruin your life, refuse to let them discourage you. Continue to live by faith, serve the Lord in your integrity, and obey the Word of God. When there is nothing else you can do, keep your eyes on the Lord and serve Him faithfully.

Lord, I pray for Your blessing on me as I work. May Your confidence and joy flood my life and be a testimony to my work team. May I work hard and profitably; use my work habits as a testimony to those who work around me. Bless me that I may bless my company with financial returns. Bless me that I may produce products or services that will bless others. Amen.

QUESTIONS FOR THOUGHT

1. Do you really believe that God wants to bless others through you, and do you believe that God will use you at your job to bless other people?

2. When God prospers your company or business, do you really think God could work through you to answer this prayer?

3. Do you believe that God has opened the door for you to be employed where you are now working? Why has God put you in your present job?

4. Are the good things that happen to you at work the blessing of God?

5. What improvements can you make at your job by praying for God's blessing on your work? On your work team? On the work that you do? And on the service you provide or the product that you make?

Chapter 12

How to Pray About Retirement

Elmer Towns

Man is so made that he can only find relaxation from one kind of labor by taking up another. —Winston Churchill

For to me, living means living for Christ, and dying is even better (Philippians 1:21 NLT).

IF you retire without a goal, it's like going bowling where there are no pins on the alley or shooting basketball without a hoop. Just hanging around the bowling lanes or basketball court gets boring if there are no games, no competition, or no winning. So retire to do something that has a purpose or accomplishes something in life. You will get bored just sitting around the house with nothing to do.

Don't retire from your job and quit living. Rather than just walking away from work that gave you life, retire to start doing another task that will give you a better and more fulfilling life.

Pray About Your Retirement Long Before You Get There

Many are not sure why they are retiring. They just do not want to work anymore; that may be the way you feel, but that's not the way to retire. One thing is always true: until you know what you want in life, where you want to go in life, and how to get where you want to go, your life will never come together.

If you were in a boat on the ocean, and you did not know which way you wanted to go, any direction may be all right. Any wind is favorable. Any tide is acceptable. But some directions lead to death, while others lead you safely in another direction. Some people retire to enter an ocean of nothingness. They let the wind blow them where it will, they let the tide take them where it desires because they have no purpose in retirement.

No wonder one of the highest mortality rates for retired people is four to six months after retirement. Could it be the physical system in the body shuts down when the mind and heart do not give it direction?

In the field of sports, the worst thing a team can do is give the ball to a player who does not know where the goal is. The worst thing in life is to retire without a goal.

Add Planning to Your Praying

People have a huge lack of motivation problem when they do not know what they want. Sometimes there are excuses: I am too old, I am too tired, I am too sick, I do not have the money, I do not have the education, or any other reasons they can think of. But one of the saddest excuses—I do not have enough time left in life. Early praying and planning solves these problems and excuses.

Retirement is not a destination, it is the journey. The problem with most people who retire is they don't have a journey to take or a place to go, they just quit working. And to that I add, they quit living.

Pray About Your Life's Goal

Long before retiring, you should be praying about your life's goal. There are many reasons why people do not achieve what they want in life. But most of the problems are on the inside, not because of their circumstances. We are not fired from our jobs, nor are we mugged by robbers, nor are we shot down by enemies, nor are we deserted by friends—the biggest problem is self-deception. We end up sabotaging ourselves.

That's why prayer about your retirement is so necessary. Remember, prayer is a relationship. As you continually talk to God about your life's goals, the issue of retirement will begin to focus clearly in your mind. And as you pray about your life after your monetary job, you'll begin to focus on what you'll do, where you'll do it, and how you'll pay for it. And beyond that, you begin to pray about new skills and knowledge how to do it.

Pray That You Don't Quit Growing

Many people do not retire from work, they just quit. When they quit working, they quit meeting someone else's standards. When they quit trying new things, they quit stretching themselves. When they quit working, they quit learning. When they quit trying new things, they quit growing.

If you are not willing to learn, you are not able to grow.

Some people go through life without a goal. Obviously, they have a goal of getting a job, making house payments, buying groceries, and having some fun each weekend. But one day the job dries up; they either get fired, or they retire. They learn a very important lesson the hard way. There is no final satisfaction going through life without having a final goal at retirement. Why? Because goals give us energy, they get us up in the morning, make us work hard; and when we reach a goal, we are fulfilled.

Every time we reach a goal, we move to a higher level of living. So retire with a goal to move to a higher level of your life.

Every person who retires should set realistic goals, if for no other reason than for the excitement they'll experience. When you set a goal, the magic begins to happen. Throw a switch, let the electricity flow. Setting a goal is like turning on the ignition in the car to start a journey.

PRAY EXCITEDLY

Setting a goal will start the imagination flowing. You may pray about working in a food kitchen serving the poor. Who knows, perhaps you'll move to the foreign mission field to be a financial accountant for mission projects, or you'll construct a church, or you'll be dorm parents in a Bible college.

MAKE THE GOLDEN YEARS GOLDEN

When you finally retire, you should achieve the dreams for which you have dreamed. Retirement should be a time when your whole life comes together. So enter retirement with prayer, and look back to thank God for all of the experiences He has given you and all the tasks you have completed. Then, pray about your daily service and challenges. Ask God to help you just as much in retirement as He did when you were working full-time. And finally, look to the future. Remember what Paul said:

> *For to me, to live is Christ, and to die is gain. But if I live on in the flesh, this will mean fruit from my labor; yet what I shall choose I cannot tell. For I am hard-pressed between the two, having a desire to depart and be with Christ, which is far better* (Philippians 1:21-23).

> *Lord, I pray for You to lead me into retirement. May I retire in Your perfect will. May my life be happier and more productive for You after I retire than when I was working. Amen.*

Know the Five Doors to Retirement

The first is the door of *expectancy*. As people face that door, they begin to dream about owning a charter fishing boat, or moving into the cottage by the lake, or playing golf every day, or living in a retirement home with many friends around them during lunch or dinner each evening. Whatever, almost everyone has some dreams of what he is going to do after his work days are over.

At their workplace, people are advised to put aside money for retirement; this advice comes from the human relations office, financial advisors, or life insurance salespeople.

You learn about this first door when you plan for retirement, gearing up for separation from the work world, and dreaming of what you will do after retirement.

The second is the *honeymoon door*. Much like a young couple getting married; most get so excited for the celebration that they have planned little for what happens after the event. Many newly married couples don't plan how they'll spend their money, who will control the money, or how they'll relate to one another. So the couple ends up arguing over money because they haven't made any financial plans for their marriage.

When you first retire, the honeymoon stage works for a couple of weeks, months, or even a couple of years. What happens when the "fun" is over? What happens when you fall out of love with retirement?

You have to do more than just plan to have fun when you retire; you must plan for daily routines, a change in your body health, and even a change in your daily strength and memory. It's important for you to know that retirement is much more than a honeymoon.

The third door is *disenchantment*. Some couples get married and become completely disenchanted with one another; those marriages lead to divorce. Perhaps the young couple didn't really know one another, didn't know what they would do for one another, and didn't plan how to relate to one another. When life's irritations rub their dreams the wrong way, divorce follows.

The same happens to the retirement honeymoon. After you finish working, you won't spend your life just sitting on the back porch sipping lemonade, doing nothing.

When we work hard, our body complains. When we use our mind constantly, stress builds up and we want relief. So it's only natural that "doing nothing" or coming to a place of complete "peace" sounds great, after all, we deserve a little "fun" after working all those years.

While the whole body may cry out for relaxation, once it gets that rest, it is ready to go back to work again. Of course in retirement work stress is reduced, but still the human soul will atrophy if it doesn't have something to do. While we think we want peace, we will probably hate the atrophy we get from it.

The fourth door is *re-orientation*. Many retirements begin with disenchantment, but no one has to live in the state of depression. If our pre-retirement dream was unrealistic, then we have to live in the nasty "now and now." But, our life doesn't have to be empty and anticlimactic.

Begin now praying about your new life's daily schedule after retirement. Put your priorities in order:

1. Personal health, grooming, and care.

2. Spiritual commitments to God.

3. Home commitments.

4. Service commitments.

5. Enjoyable activities.

Pray about each of these activities, and ask God to give you wisdom to balance your new life and the diversified challenges it brings to you. Ask God to help you make the proper investment in each of these activities. Probably you will find great peace and confidence in a balanced life after you retire.

The fifth door is *stability*. Perhaps your entire life has been gearing up toward "retirement." What happens when you get there? Just as you prioritized your tasks when you were at work, now you must continue to prioritize your tasks. All tasks are not work related; you must build a sense of destiny and fulfillment into each day. Whatever you do, make sure you do it for Jesus Christ.

> *Work willingly at whatever you do, as though you were working for the Lord rather than for people. Remember that the Lord will give you an inheritance as your reward, and that the Master you are serving is Christ* (Colossians 3:23-24 NLT).

> *Lord, help me understand the five doors to retirement and make plans for them now. Give me wisdom to see beyond the last day of work, and give me wisdom to plan for my life beyond the last day of formal work. I will learn, plan, provide, and look forward to retirement. Amen.*

Financial Planning

Audit Your Finances Every Year

Even when you are young, take a little time each year to assess your financial situation, especially looking to the future. Focus on where you are, where you want to be when you retire, and how much time you have left to plan for retirement. Then begin putting money and assets in place to make it happen. This may be an unpleasant task for some because you love to work and you're afraid of not working.

But remember what your mother told you, "You have to eat your vegetables before you can eat dessert." And what does that mean? First, you have to plan for your retirement and work hard for your retirement by putting aside money. That's eating your vegetables first. Dessert comes later, which will be retirement.

Take Advantage of Known Resources

You'll want to know what Social Security benefits will do for you, what your retirement package will do for you, what your personal investment portfolio will do for you, how much life insurance you have to take care of your death or your spouse after you die, and what Medicare, Medicaid, and healthcare costs you have.

You have to educate yourself about your own retirement because no one else is going to do it for you. You may get some help from your employer, union, church, or non-profit groups, but in the final analysis only you know what is best for you.

Lord, remind me that money is life, and help me manage my money as I manage my life. I will plan financially for the future, and I will audit my finances each year so I'll have a productive retirement that will bring glory to You. Amen.

MAKING POSITIVE PLANS FOR RETIREMENT

Just as you go through your financial retirement portfolio, how about going through your psychological portfolio, or even better, go through your spiritual portfolio. Take the following steps:

Retire to Do Something

As it has been said throughout this chapter, make sure there is purpose in retirement, for then you'll find happiness and satisfaction. Remember, happiness is found on the road to duty.

I remember years ago a beauty queen being quizzed for the crown; she was asked what was the purpose of life. She answered, "Happiness…just to be happy!" I said at the time that girl will never find happiness for she probably thinks happiness comes as you sit around doing nothing. Again, "happiness is found on the road to duty." The better you accomplish things in life, the happier you will be.

Practice Being Retired

You'll have time to take vacations throughout your life; practice just being at home with nothing to do. Yes, most of us will enjoy doing nothing for a day or two, or even a week or two; but after awhile, it gets humdrum. So use your vacations to practice being retired.

Don't forget that there are trips to take on your vacation; think about becoming a world traveler after you retire. If you have enough finances to take a few trips, congratulations.

Realize That Expectations Change

As you get older, your kids and grandkids will expect you to babysit; after all, they think you have absolutely "nothing to do." You'll be expected to help them save on babysitting and childcare expenses or other costs. Some will want you to run errands for them or a dozen other things they don't have time to do. Plan your life with a purpose, and let them know your schedule. Let them know your boundaries and what you can't or won't do.

You may want to do these things as a ministry to your family; others will have to do it because of financial difficulties. And others will want to do it because they just enjoy looking after children. The bottom line—people will have expectations for your "free time." So if you don't plan what you're going to do with your time, somebody else will fill it up for you.

Anticipate New Skills

Retirement will be a great time to attend classes for the new challenges in your life. You may want to do something entirely different from what you've been doing in the past or at work. This is your opportunity to take courses, complete a college degree, or acquire a new skill. You can join a sports league, become involved in Christian service activities, or even take on a part-time ministry position at your church.

Prepare for a Self-identity Change

Most people don't realize when they give up their work, they will change their self-perception. Most people who work see themselves as a bank teller, truck driver, or veterinarian. Don't most people identify their self-perception with their vocational role? So what's going to happen when you don't have a vocation?

You can't tell people that "I used to work at a bank" or "I used to be a dentist." (Aren't you still a dentist even if you don't maintain your practice?)

Those who have been in positions of power and authority will have difficulty identifying themselves without identifying with their previous vocation.

Think of how you're going to introduce yourself to others. What do you say? "I'm retired" or will you say, "I'm a former postal worker." Obviously, you can't say to people: "I'm a millionaire" nor can you say to them, "I'm self-employed" that is, if you're not self-employed.

Expect Changes in Relationships

You have had many relationships in life. You interact with people at church, your workplace, and perhaps in a sports league. Then there are relationships in the neighborhood, among the extended family, and at many other places in life.

When you change your basic self-perception and retire, people will relate to you differently. You need to face the question: "How will I relate to people when I have extra time, and I don't have a job?" How will I relate to those I used to work with?

You will have a different relationship to your spouse. Perhaps when you had a job, everything in the home took second place because you were the breadwinner. But now, the bread has already been won, and you don't need your job to keep the household going.

So "turf issues" may be a challenge. Who gets to use the telephone? Computer? Television? Run the errands? Again, we face the expectation: "What does the family expect me to do for them now that I have more time?" Babysitting, other projects from the family—you should settle these issues before retirement.

Prepare for a Life Purpose Change

Before you retired, you were expected to be at the office, or to make sales presentations, or to be at the construction site early, but with retirement those expectations change. Sometimes you had to produce things with your hands—type pages, assemble parts, or drive a taxi. But now you don't. No one demands the skills that you have acquired, so you don't feel as needed. Sometimes if we don't feel needed, our self-worth goes out the window.

So what must you do? *Expect* changes in your life's purpose. Therefore, make sure you retire with a purpose and goal.

Lord, I plan to live for You after I no longer work at a job. Help me plan for the future just as I plan now for each day. May I serve You effectively in the future, as I am today. Amen.

Questions to Answer Before Retirement

Many people plan for their retirement when only a year or two away. However, the following questions should help you *pray* about your retirement; and best of all, *plan* for your retirement.

+ Where will you live?

+ When will you want to make a move to that place?

+ Should your automobile be replaced before retirement?

+ Are there major household repairs or replacements to make before retirement?

- How are you going to pay your present monthly debt after retirement?

- Will you be able to negotiate any loans from investment institutions after retirement?

- Can you pay off all your indebtedness (except house) before retirement?

- Do you have an accurate picture of your monthly expenses before retirement and after retirement?

- How much less can you live on after retirement?

- How many expenses relating to your employment will be eliminated at retirement (commuting to work, clothing, meals, dues, fees, etc.)?

- How much exercise will you get after retirement?

- What *stuff* will you get rid of as you retire? Before you retire? (Should you begin giving away or selling a lot of your stuff before retirement?)

- How much money will you need for special events after retirement? (Christmas gifts, Valentine gifts, birthday, anniversaries, tithe, etc.)

- How much money do you want to leave to your family as a legacy, how little do you want to have when you die?

- Is it possible to ease into retirement over several years rather than one sudden change that will affect you mentally, physically, and spiritually?

PLAN TO CREATE A NEW ROUTINE

You can't suddenly stop doing something you've done every day; it's jarring to the equilibrium. As a matter of fact, most of us have a daily routine and when we "stop" work, it upsets our personality. Professor Chris Sharpley, who heads the Centre for Stress Management and Research in Monash University, Australia, says, "Men experience a 'retirement letdown' after six months while women don't experience that problem until five years after retirement."[1] He thinks perhaps it might be because of the demands placed upon the woman by their aging husbands.

Before you retire, sketch out what you think may be a daily routine for you. You may get up earlier in the morning, which means you'll be tired in the evening and go to bed earlier. If you get up early, what will you do with that time? If you don't have a schedule for retirement, you'll be living without anything to do. Like it or not, our self-perception is enhanced by our self-work.

You ought to make a list of things you plan to do. Keep the list visible so you can pray about it. Having a list enhances the excitement of retirement. Plan to:

- Learn games, or recapture games you've played earlier in life.

- Work in the garden or tend to house plants.

- Upgrade the landscape around the home.

- Redecorate or reconfigure your house.

- Travel.

- Work a part-time job to supplement your income.

- ◆ Work at the church.

- ◆ Enroll in adult education or online courses.

- ◆ Resume a former hobby and block out time each day to work on it.

- ◆ Join a health club or exercise class.

- ◆ Volunteer in community activities, church activities.

- ◆ Include grandchildren, family, and extended family in your life.

WRONG PLANS

One of the worst things you can do after retirement is to use your retirement as an excuse to stop being Christian, serving at the church, tithing, or using your spiritual gifts for the advancement of the Kingdom.

Then there's a second thing. Some people think that at retirement they can now become "selfish" because this is *their* time of life. They may stop serving at the church, stop helping others, and think only of themselves.

So what can you do? Remember the exhortation of Jesus, *"Be faithful until death, and I will give you the crown of life"* (Rev. 2:10). Plan to keep doing for Christ what you are doing now, even though you may do it differently, at a different speed, and at a different level.

As I write this chapter, I am 77 years of age and I love serving Christ as much now as I ever have before. I know that with advanced age I am not as strong as I used to be, so I've learned to manage my strength. I can work as hard as I used to work, but I can't work as long. So, I manage to work in spurts, and rest a little longer between the tasks.

When you realize you have limited strength, you have a great advantage over your weaknesses. Al Worthington, former World Series pitcher for the New York Giants and Minnesota Twins, was asked, "Al...can you still throw the fastball as hard as you did when you were in the World Series?" Al answered, "Yes...but it takes longer to get to the plate."

You may laugh, but it's good to know what you can't do and how you've changed. That puts you in control of your life.

Manage Your Time

If you were an effective worker at your job, then you've probably learned to manage your time and to get the most done each day. In the same way, now that you are retired, you must learn to manage your time to get the most out of life each day. Whether you're working or retired, God still tells you to *"redeem the time"* (Eph. 5:16; Col. 4:5). And what does it mean to "redeem"? It means to "buy back." When you pawn something at a pawn shop, you must go and buy it back so you can use it again. So let's "buy back" our time so we may use it properly in retirement.

Pray Positively for Your Retirement

No matter what happens to you after retirement, you can't plan for everything, nor can you anticipate every event. There will be some "wins" and some "losses." Since you don't know what they will be, you can plan to be positive about life and positive to what the Lord will bring into your life.

I've written frequently that, "You can't choose what will happen to you, but you can choose how you will respond."

If you choose how you will respond to the problems in retirement, you'll be positive and in control. But if you become a pawn dictated by the things that happen to you, you'll be blindsided by every negative feeling that comes along.

Lord, I look forward to retirement because I know it will happen one day if Jesus doesn't come or I don't come home in death. Now, Lord, help me plan for my retirement. Help me put aside finances, realistic expectations, and assets for my retirement.

I want to serve You when I retire. I want to be more effective for You in the future than I've been in the past. Help me grow today, and every tomorrow until I reach retirement. Then use me abundantly, as fully as You can.

Thank You for my life, my family, my salvation, and opportunities to serve You. I look forward to the future with optimism. Amen.

Questions for Thought

1. When should you begin praying about retirement, and how often should you pray about it?

2. What kind of financial planning should you do for your retirement (life insurance, securities, retirement funds, real estate holdings, owned businesses, etc.)?

3. How much is enough money for retirement?

4. What would you like to do for God when you retire that you are not doing now?

5. What hobbies or activities would you like to take up after you retire?

6. What should couples talk about when planning retirement?

7. What should/could you do for your retired relatives who can't support themselves?

Endnote

1. See Chuck Gallozzi, *Preparing for Retirement*, available at http://www.personal-development.com/chuck/retirement. htm (accessed November 12, 2009).

Epilogue

Elmer Towns

If you wouldn't work so hard to get out of work, then you
would only work half as hard as you have to work. But
when you work too fast, and you take shortcuts, and you do
it half way, you'll probably end up coming back and having
to do it again—which means you'll have to work twice as
hard than if you would have done it right the first time.
—Elmer Towns

Pay careful attention to your own work, for then you will
get the satisfaction of a job well done, and you won't need
to compare yourself to anyone else (Galatians 6:4 NLT).

THERE is a difference between work and employment. It all has to do with attitude. Work is what you do because you want to do it, while employment is doing something you have to do to get paid.

As an illustration, I have taught the Pastor's Bible Class at my church for 23 years, and I don't get paid. It's work I love to do, and I look forward to doing it every week. I love to do this just as much as many other Sunday school teachers all over the world love their work.

Some people hate their job, so it becomes demeaning and demoralizing. They come away from their jobs angry, bitter, or perhaps with broken health or broken spirits.

This reminds me of an uncle who once told me how to have a successful life:

"Find a job you love to do where they'll pay you, and you'll never have to work another day in your life."

I once had a job I hated. I was attending Dallas Theological Seminary full time, taking Greek, Hebrew, and systematic theology. I had to write term papers—long term papers. My professors thought a term paper shorter than 30 pages didn't deserve an "A." Those papers took a lot of time.

Several of my classmates were "elite scholars." They didn't have jobs, so they got to study and enjoy their time at Dallas. I had a job. My days were long and arduous; I got up at six in the morning and went to bed after midnight. I spent one year at Republic National Bank writing insurance for all the important papers mailed from the bank. My job included doing "stuff" I didn't want to do, and I wasn't learning anything; all I got was money for my effort. The following year I was transferred and became a night deposit teller, balancing deposits left in the depository.

The figures almost never balanced. The problem was other people's mistakes, plus I had an old-fashioned adding machine with a long metal arm to pull. Every night I had to stay until I found the mistakes, and that was on my own time. I hated the fact that I had to put in anywhere from one to three hours of my own time in the evenings. I would have rather been at home writing a term paper or watching television with my young, growing family. But I was stuck at my job; being punished for other people's mistakes.

I really hated that job! I felt that I was wasting my time, wasting my youth—but I did earn money to pay our bills. It was a job I hated but employment I needed.

Sometimes your work deals with career, and at other times your work deals with compassion (reduce compassion to a minimum and it becomes passion). You work at your career because it's expected, and you work at your passion because it's what you want to do.

Some work is servitude (you're the one in bondage), while other work is service to others, which is enjoyable. You may hate bondage, but you love compassion.

Working your career is an occupation done for money; working your passion is an opportunity to do what you want to do.

I am 77 years old and thank God daily that I can wake up every morning with an opportunity to go to work for God. I get to teach champions for Christ at Liberty University. Beyond that, I have renewed stamina every morning so that I want to go to work. Isn't that wonderful?

Sometimes, your career is motivated by finances, you do it for money. But on the other hand, sometimes you have a completely different motive. You're being faithful. You don't do it primarily for money; you do it for Christ.

Sometimes a dentist gets boxed into his occupation of filling cavities and pulling teeth. He does it for finances; he feels that the office is where he fulfills his services; dentistry is his career.

But then the dentist goes on a mission trip with his church to a primitive nation. Now his dentistry is transformed and becomes the greatest motivation in his life. He realizes that Christ can use him to make a huge difference in the lives of the poor as he heals diseases, eliminates pain, and makes faces beautiful. His only pay is a big, toothy smile. Now his passion is people, and he's serving the Lord through his occupation.

The Obligation of Prayer

Notice how you pray differently for a job than you do for things you enjoy doing. A job is something you have to do, so you pray that God blesses your work. You feel the burden of prayer because you must do your job, and you must do your best.

Your job demands excellence, and there are huge consequences in the balance. If you don't do your employment well, you lose money, you get fired, and there are consequences at home if you can't pay your bills. Many times some will pray more about their employment for money than they pray for their passion of serving others.

So how should we pray? Suppose your job description is changed. They want you to come earlier, do it differently, or go in a different direction. Because you have committed yourself to that job, you pray to be flexible. You commit your new routine to God and ask Him to bless the work of your hands.

But not all people pray about their jobs. Sometimes a union member yells to a union steward, "They can't do that to me!" But suppose you're not a union member; you go to the coffee room and complain to the other team members, "They can't do that to me!" So both the job we hate and the service we love needs prayer.

But we'll probably approach prayer differently, because one involves our relationship to Christ, as opposed to the other that involves our livelihood. Yet in both can we pray with a sour attitude? Can we expect God to use us when we have a rebellious spirit?

First we need to pray for ourselves before we pray about the things we do in our work.

Getting a Better Attitude About Work

A defining moment took place in my life when I was around nine-years-old. I had to cut the grass at my home in Savannah, Georgia. The front yard was sectioned off to three small plots of grass, about the size of a bathroom. The same with the side yard, except they were long, narrow strips of grass like a hallway. The backyard was about the size of a kitchen.

I hated to mow the grass, so when I had to do it, I would mow only one portion, sit and rest awhile and drink some iced tea. It's called procrastination. I put off what I didn't want to do. As a result, it took all afternoon to cut the grass, and I rarely did a good job.

One fall afternoon, all of my buddies came over to play football in the plowed field owned by Sergeant Sullivan next to our home. We couldn't run very fast in the deeply plowed dirt, nor could we pass the ball very far; but we sure enjoyed tackling one another in soft dirt and piling on. Needless to say, we got filthy dirty.

When I asked to play football that day, "No," my mother told me, I couldn't play. "No. I've asked you for the past two days to cut the grass and you kept putting it off. It must be mowed today."

"But, Mother, I want to play with the boys."

Mother would hear none of my pleas, so while the guys were yelling, laughing, and tackling one another in the soft dirt, I was within earshot; mowing the grass and hating every moment of my servitude.

We all finished about the same time, so the boys came over to lay on my freshly cut grass. A garden hose poured fresh water over our dirty bodies. We washed, then lay in the sun to dry off, laughing about any and every thing.

Then it dawned on me, I hurt because of pushing the lawnmower, and the boys hurt from all the tackling. I was filthy from work, they were filthy from football. They worked as hard as I did, but I hated it while they laughed and enjoyed it.

Lying in the sun that afternoon changed my life. I came to the conclusion that there was not much difference between hard work and hard play. I thought if I made work "fun," life would be much happier.

About a week or so later, I again had to cut the grass. I went straight outside and cut all seven patches of grass without stopping. When I finished, I manicured the edges with clippers, then poured water all over my body and again lay in the sun. This time I was as happy as if I were playing football.

And what is the bottom line? You can have fun as you work, or you *can fuss*. The difference is attitude.

My granddaughter, Beth Wooldridge, read the above story when she was about ten-years-old, and came to a family dinner to announce, "Doc, I know why you're a workaholic!"

Everyone at the table stared at her, as though she said something wrong. Then she said, "Do you know that people call you a workaholic behind your back?"

I smiled and said, "They do? Why?"

"Because you make work fun."

She went on to say that I must really get a lot of pleasure out of working. And then came the best part of the whole conversation, "I'm going to be like you when I grow up, I'm going to make work fun."

Conclusion

Your attitude toward work is more important than your skills or strengths. Make your work fun, and you'll enjoy life a lot more.

About Dr. Elmer Towns

Dr. Elmer Towns is an author of popular and scholarly works, a seminar lecturer, and dedicated worker in Sunday school. He has written over 130 books, including several best sellers. He won the coveted Gold Medallion Book Award for *The Names of the Holy Spirit*.

Dr. Towns cofounded Liberty University with Jerry Falwell in 1971 and now serves as dean of the B.R. Lakin School of Religion and as distinguished professor of Theology and New Testament.

Liberty University was founded in 1971 and is the fastest-growing Christian university in America. Located in Lynchburg, Virginia, Liberty University is a private, coeducational, undergraduate and graduate institution offering 38 undergraduate and 15 graduate programs serving over 35,000 resident and external students (12,700 on campus). Individuals from all 50 states and more than 70 nations compose the diverse student body. While the faculty and students vary greatly, the common denominator and driving force of Liberty University since its conception is love for Jesus Christ and the desire to make Him known to the entire world.

For more information about Liberty University, contact:

Liberty University
1971 University Boulevard
Lynchburg, VA 24502
Telephone: 434-582-2000
Website: www.Liberty.edu

About Dr. David Earley

Dr. Dave Earley is Chairman of the Department of Pastoral Leadership at Liberty Baptist Theological Seminary and Liberty University. He also serves as Director of the Center for Ministry Training at Liberty Baptist Theological Seminary, and the Director of the Center for Church Planting of Liberty University. Dave received his education at Liberty University and Liberty Theological Seminary and was awarded the Doctor of Ministry degree.

Dave has written 15 books, including *Prayer Odyssey* and *Praying For Your Children*.

Dave served as the founding senior pastor of the New Life Church of Gahanna, a church which started in his basement with 12 people and grew to nearly 2,000 a week in attendance. New Life has been recognized as one of the healthiest churches in America with over 70% of the members involved in ministry and over a 100 small groups. Since 1999, New Life has intentionally mothered five healthy new churches.

Dave and his wife, Cathy, have three sons who are all studying ministry at Liberty University.

IN THE RIGHT HANDS, THIS BOOK WILL CHANGE LIVES!

Most of the people who need this message will not be looking for this book. To change their lives, you need to put a copy of this book in their hands.

> *But others (seeds) fell into good ground, and brought forth fruit, some a hundred-fold, some sixty-fold, some thirty-fold* (Matthew 13:8).

Our ministry is constantly seeking methods to find the good ground, the people who need this anointed message to change their lives. Will you help us reach these people?

> *Remember this—a farmer who plants only a few seeds will get a small crop. But the one who plants generously will get a generous crop* (2 Corinthians 9:6).

EXTEND THIS MINISTRY BY SOWING
3 BOOKS, 5 BOOKS, 10 BOOKS, **OR MORE TODAY,**
AND BECOME A LIFE CHANGER!

Thank you,

Don Nori Sr., Publisher
Destiny Image
Since 1982

DESTINY IMAGE PUBLISHERS, INC.

*"Speaking to the Purposes of God for This Generation
and for the Generations to Come."*

VISIT OUR NEW SITE HOME AT
WWW.DESTINYIMAGE.COM

FREE SUBSCRIPTION TO DI NEWSLETTER

Receive free unpublished articles by top DI authors, exclusive

discounts, and free downloads from our best and newest books.

Visit www.destinyimage.com to subscribe.

Write to: Destiny Image
             P.O. Box 310
             Shippensburg, PA 17257-0310

Call: 1-800-722-6774

Email: orders@destinyimage.com

For a complete list of our titles or to place an order
online, visit www.destinyimage.com.

FIND US ON FACEBOOK OR FOLLOW US ON TWITTER.

www.facebook.com/destinyimage   facebook
www.twitter.com/destinyimage   twitter